Oodles & Oodles of Ramen Noodles

Surprising & delicious ways to use your noodle!

Printed in the United States of America
by G&R Publishing Co.

Distributed By:

CQProducts

507 Industrial Street
Waverly, IA 50677

ISBN-13: 978-1-56383-373-1
ISBN-10: 1-56383-373-5
Item #7060

Table of Contents

Using Your Noodle

What makes ramen so special?

The low cost, convenience and versatility – and perhaps the wavy curls! These instant noodles are perfect for fast-paced lives.

Each inexpensive cellophane package holds a block of thin curly noodles and includes a small packet of seasoning. The many different seasoning flavors lend a distinctive taste to the standard ramen noodle. The noodles cook quickly in boiling water, about 3 minutes, and the seasoning turns plain water into a flavorful broth for an instant meal. It's easy to toss in vegetables, meat or other ingredients to add bulk and nutrition to the soup.

But ramen noodles go far beyond a poor man's porridge. They can dress up any dish, with or without the seasoning packets. Uncooked and broken into pieces, these noodles add crunch to salads and desserts. When browned in a skillet, they add a nutty flavor to main or side dishes. And ramen noodles can be a quick-fix replacement for other types of pasta.

In some recipes, the seasoning packets will not be used. They can be discarded, or better yet, saved for use in a different recipe. Use the seasoning to spice up plain cooked rice, egg noodles, soups, roasted meats or other dishes and turn them into something special.

Versatility like this is ideal for busy cooks who are short on time and money but want tasty food. No wonder ramen noodles enjoy a beloved reputation with college students!

Tips to remember:

- Uncooked noodles may be broken or crushed while still in the package or left intact in blocks.

- Cook ramen noodles just until strands separate and become tender. Overcooking results in mushy noodles that fall apart.

- For stovetop cooking, add noodles to boiling water and cook about 3 minutes.

- For microwave cooking, heat water in a microwave-safe container for 3 to 4 minutes. Add noodles and cook for about 1½ minutes.

- To brown ramen, heat oil or butter in a skillet. Break noodles into small pieces and add to the skillet. Cook and stir constantly until golden brown.

Soups

Egg Drop Ramen Soup

Makes 1 serving

Ingredients

1 carrot, sliced

4 fresh mushrooms, sliced

1 (3 oz.) pkg. ramen noodles
with seasoning packet,
any flavor

1 egg, lightly beaten

¼ C. milk

Preparation

In a medium saucepan over high heat, bring 2½ cups water to a
boil. Add carrot and boil for 7 minutes. Add mushrooms. Break
up noodles and add to saucepan with seasoning from packet;
stir to blend. Reduce heat to medium and simmer for 3 minutes
or until noodles and mushrooms are tender. Slowly pour in the
egg and stir for 30 seconds until egg has cooked. Stir in the milk
and serve hot.

** For lower sodium content, boil noodles in reduced-sodium chicken
or beef broth and omit seasoning packet.*

Meatball Soup

Makes 4 to 6 servings

Ingredients

½ lb. lean ground beef

¼ C. plain dry bread crumbs

1 egg white

1 T. minced fresh ginger

1½ tsp. low-sodium soy sauce

2 tsp. minced garlic

8 oz. baby-cut carrots, halved diagonally

2 (3 oz.) pkgs. Oriental flavor ramen noodles with seasoning packets

8 oz. fresh broccoli florets

6 oz. fresh sugar snap peas, stems and strings removed

2 tsp. dark sesame oil

Green onions, sliced

Preparation

In a medium bowl, combine ground beef, bread crumbs, egg white, ginger, soy sauce and garlic, mixing with hands as needed until well blended. Place mixture on waxed paper and pat into a 6″ square. Cut into 36 (1″) squares and roll each square into a ball; set aside. In a large saucepan over high heat, bring 5 cups water to a boil. Add carrots to boiling water, reduce heat to medium and cook for 4 to 5 minutes or until almost tender. Add meatballs to saucepan, one at a time. Add seasoning from one or both packets, according to taste; stir. Add broccoli, reduce heat to a simmer, cover and cook for 6 to 7 minutes, until vegetables are tender. Break noodles into four pieces; add to soup and cook for 1 minute, stirring to separate noodles. Stir in peas and boil gently for 2 minutes or until noodles are tender and peas turn bright green. Stir in oil, remove from heat and divide among serving bowls. Garnish with sliced onion.

Santa Fe Soup

Makes 4 to 6 servings

Ingredients

1 T. olive oil

6 oz. lean pork, cut into thin strips

1 tomato, chopped

1 (14 oz.) can golden hominy with liquid

1 (4 oz.) can whole roasted chilies, drained and chopped

2 (3 oz.) pkgs. beef or picante beef flavor ramen noodles with seasoning packets

Tortilla chips, broken

Sliced green onions

Preparation

In a large saucepan over medium-high heat, heat oil. Add pork and cook until browned, stirring often. Add 4 cups water, tomato, hominy with liquid, chilies, noodles and seasoning from both packets. Bring mixture to a boil and cook until noodles are tender, about 3 minutes. Garnish with tortilla chips and green onions before serving.

Ramen Corn Chowder

Makes 4 servings

Ingredients

1 (3 oz.) pkg. chicken flavor ramen noodles with seasoning packet
1 (15 oz.) can cream style corn
1 C. frozen whole kernel corn

¼ tsp. ground ginger
½ tsp. curry powder
½ C. milk
½ C. shredded Colby cheese

Preparation

In a large saucepan over medium heat, bring 2 cups water to a boil. Break up noodles slightly. Add noodles and seasoning from packet to boiling water and cook for 3 minutes. Add canned corn, frozen corn, ginger, curry powder and milk; bring mixture to a gentle simmer and cook for 2 to 4 minutes but do not boil. Add cheese and stir until melted and soup is well blended. Serve immediately.

Variation: Add ¼ cup cooked crumbled bacon and/or ¼ cup chopped sautéed onions to the soup when adding corn and other ingredients. For thinner soup, add more milk.

Southwest Shrimp & Noodle Soup

Makes 4 to 6 servings

Ingredients

1 lb. shrimp, peeled and deveined (fresh or frozen)

1 T. lemon juice

¼ tsp. chili powder

¼ tsp. ground cumin

⅛ tsp. pepper

2 (3 oz.) pkgs. shrimp or Oriental flavor ramen noodles with 1 seasoning packet

2 C. salsa

1 (15 oz.) can black beans, rinsed and drained

1 (11 oz.) can whole kernel or shoepeg corn with liquid

1 green onion, sliced

Preparation

If shrimp is frozen, rinse in cool water until thawed; set aside. In a medium bowl, stir together lemon juice, chili powder, cumin and pepper. Add shrimp and toss to coat; let stand for 20 minutes. Meanwhile, in a large saucepan over high heat, bring 5 cups water to a boil. Stir in seasoning from one packet; discard remaining packet or reserve for another use. Break up noodles and add to saucepan; return to a boil and cook for 1 minute. Add shrimp mixture, salsa, beans, corn with liquid and onion; heat through until shrimp turn pink. Serve immediately.

Asian Chicken Noodle Soup

Makes 3 to 4 servings

Ingredients

2 (14 oz.) cans chicken broth

1 T. soy sauce

1 tsp. grated fresh ginger

⅛ tsp. crushed red pepper flakes

1 red bell pepper, cored and cut into ¾″ pieces

1 carrot, chopped

⅓ C. thinly sliced green onions

1 (3 oz.) pkg. ramen noodles, any flavor

1 C. chopped cooked chicken

1 C. fresh halved snow peas or ½ (6 oz.) pkg. frozen snow peas, thawed and halved

Preparation

In a large saucepan over medium heat, combine 1 cup water, broth, soy sauce, ginger and red pepper flakes. Bring mixture to a boil. Add bell pepper, carrot and onions. Return to boiling and then reduce heat. Cover and simmer for 4 to 6 minutes or until vegetables are crisp-tender. Remove seasoning packet from ramen package and reserve for another use. Break up noodles and add to saucepan. Stir in chicken and pea pods; simmer for 2 minutes or until noodles are tender and pea pods are crisp-tender.

Turkey Noodle Soup

Makes 5 servings

Ingredients

3 C. reduced-sodium chicken broth

1½ C. chopped cooked turkey

1 C. thinly sliced carrots

1 onion, cut into thin wedges

½ C. thinly sliced celery

1 tsp. dried thyme

1 yellow summer squash, quartered lengthwise and sliced (about 1⅓ C.)

2 (3 oz.) pkgs. chicken flavor ramen noodles with 1 seasoning packet, seasoning optional

2 T. lemon juice

Preparation

In a large saucepan over medium heat, combine 2¼ cups water, broth, turkey, carrots, onion, celery and thyme. Bring mixture to a boil. Reduce heat; cover and simmer for 15 minutes. Add squash and cook, uncovered, for 7 to 9 minutes or until vegetables are nearly crisp-tender. Add noodles and half the seasoning from one packet, if desired; discard remaining seasoning or reserve for another use. Cook for 2 minutes. Stir in lemon juice and cook 1 minute longer or until noodles are tender. Serve promptly.

Simply Creamy Mushroom Soup

Makes 2 servings

Ingredients

3 T. butter
1 clove garlic minced
½ C. chopped onion
2 C. fresh mushrooms, sliced
¼ tsp. ground thyme

1 (3 oz.) pkg. chicken flavor ramen noodles with seasoning packet
1 C. half & half
1 T. chopped fresh parsley

Preparation

In a medium saucepan over medium-low heat, melt butter. Add garlic, onion and mushrooms; sauté until onions are transparent and mushrooms are soft. Add 1 cup water, thyme and seasoning from packet; stir until blended. Stir in half & half. Cook until heated through but do not boil. Break up noodles and add to soup. Cook for 4 to 5 minutes or until tender. Stir in parsley just before serving.

Hot 'n Spicy Tempura

Makes 2 servings

Ingredients

2 breaded fish fillets

1 tsp. ginger-garlic paste*

1 (3 oz.) pkg. Oriental or shrimp flavor ramen noodles with seasoning packet

½ C. frozen Chinese stir-fry vegetables, any type

1 tsp. sesame oil

Chili powder to taste

1 green onion, thinly sliced

1 tsp. sesame seeds, toasted**

Preparation

Prepare fish according to package directions. Meanwhile, in a large saucepan over high heat, bring 3 cups water to a boil. Reduce heat and add ginger-garlic paste, coarsely broken noodles, seasoning from packet and vegetables; stir to blend. Cook for 2 minutes. Remove saucepan from heat and stir in oil. Pour mixture into a large soup bowl and sprinkle with chili powder; stir gently until blended. Place cooked fish on top of soup and garnish with onion and sesame seeds. Serve immediately.

* To make ginger-garlic paste, place 2″ fresh ginger in a food processor with 6 to 8 peeled cloves garlic; blend to paste consistency.

** To toast, place sesame seeds in a single layer on a baking sheet. Bake at 350° for approximately 6 to 8 minutes or until sesame seeds are brown.

Broccoli-Garlic Soup

Makes 2 servings

Ingredients

1 (3.5 oz.) pkg. Sapporo Ichiban original flavor ramen noodles with seasoning packet

Crushed red pepper flakes to taste

4 cloves garlic, minced

1 tsp. minced fresh ginger

⅔ C. chopped fresh or frozen broccoli florets

Preparation

In a medium saucepan over high heat, bring 3 cups water to a boil. Add block of noodles and red pepper flakes; set aside seasoning packet for later use. Cook noodles until almost tender, about 2 minutes. Reduce heat to medium high. Add garlic, ginger, seasoning from packet and broccoli. Cook until broccoli is tender, 6 to 8 minutes. Serve hot.

Cheesy Broccoli-Chicken Soup

Makes 6 to 8 servings

Ingredients

1 (16 oz.) pkg. frozen broccoli

2 (3 oz.) pkgs. cream of chicken ramen noodles with seasoning packets

¼ tsp. garlic powder

1½ C. diced cooked chicken

3 to 4 slices American cheese, cut up

Preparation

In a large saucepan, bring 5 cups water to a boil. Add broccoli and return to a boil. Cover pan, reduce heat and simmer for 3 minutes. Return to a boil. Break up noodles and add to boiling water; set seasoning packets aside for later use. Cook noodles and broccoli for 3 minutes more, stirring occasionally. Add garlic powder, chicken and seasoning from both packets. When heated through, remove pan from heat and add cheese; stir until cheese is melted and mixture is well blended. Serve immediately.

Creamy Tomato-Hot Dog Soup

Makes 2 servings

Ingredients

1 (10.7 oz.) can condensed
   tomato soup
1 soup can milk
1 carrot, chopped
1 (3 oz.) pkg. chicken flavor
   ramen noodles with
   seasoning packet

2 hot dogs, sliced
¼ C. shredded
   mozzarella cheese

Preparation

In a medium saucepan over medium-low heat, combine soup
and milk; whisk together until smooth. Add carrot and cook for
about 5 minutes, stirring frequently. Break up noodles and add
to soup mixture along with half of the seasoning from packet;
discard remaining seasoning or reserve for another use. Add hot
dog slices. Cook until noodles and carrots are tender and soup is
heated through. Pour into serving bowls and sprinkle mozzarella
cheese on top.

Szechuan Ramen Noodle Soup

Makes 3 to 4 servings

Ingredients

1 tsp. soy sauce, or to taste

1 pinch Szechwan pepper

1½ tsp. black vinegar

3 green onions, chopped

3 cloves garlic, minced,
 or to taste

Cayenne pepper oil* to taste

1 to 2 T. canola oil

Salt to taste

2 (3 oz.) pkgs. chicken flavor
 ramen noodles with
 1 seasoning packet

2 C. chopped bok choy

Preparation

To make the sauce, in a medium bowl, combine soy sauce, Szechwan pepper, vinegar, onions, garlic, pepper oil and canola oil; mix well. Season with salt, if desired. In a medium saucepan over medium-high heat, bring 4 cups water to a boil. Stir in seasoning from one packet; discard remaining packet or reserve for another use. Break up noodles slightly and add to boiling water; cook for 2 minutes or until almost tender. Add bok choy and cook for 3 minutes longer or until vegetables are slightly softened. Pour mixture into bowl with sauce and stir. Serve immediately.

To make cayenne pepper oil, heat 1 to 2 tablespoons canola oil in a small saucepan over medium-high heat until almost smoking; stir in 1 to 2 teaspoons ground cayenne pepper and cook until fragrant. Cool before use.

Shiitake Noodle Soup

Makes 2 to 4 servings

Ingredients

½ C. shiitake mushrooms

1 (3 oz.) pkg. mushroom flavor ramen noodles with seasoning packet

Preparation

In a large saucepan, combine 4 cups water and mushrooms; allow mushrooms to soak for 30 minutes without heat. Then place saucepan over medium heat and bring mixture to a boil. Turn off heat, cover and allow mushrooms to soak in hot water for 30 minutes. Remove mushrooms from broth and set aside to keep warm. Return saucepan to medium heat and stir in part or all of the seasoning from packet. Bring mixture to a boil. Break up noodles and add to saucepan. Boil noodles for 3 minutes or until tender. Add mushrooms and stir until heated through. Serve immediately.

Variation: Add bamboo shoots, chopped scallions and chopped green bell pepper, cooking until tender.

Slow Cooker Oriental Chicken Soup

Makes 6 to 8 servings

Ingredients

1¼ lbs. boneless, skinless chicken thighs

1 (16 oz.) pkg. baby-cut carrots, sliced lengthwise

½ C. chopped celery

1 (8 oz.) can sliced bamboo shoots, drained

1 (8 oz.) can sliced water chestnuts, drained

1 (3 oz.) pkg. Oriental flavor ramen noodles with seasoning packet

1 (32 oz.) carton reduced-sodium chicken broth

1 C. frozen sugar snap peas

2 green onions, sliced

Pepper to taste, optional

Preparation

In a 3½- to 4-quart slow cooker, place chicken pieces. In layers, add carrots, celery, bamboo shoots and water chestnuts. Sprinkle seasoning from packet over layers; reserve noodles for later use. Pour broth over the top of layers, cover slow cooker and cook on low setting for 7 to 8 hours. Approximately 20 minutes before serving, rinse peas to thaw; set aside. Remove chicken from slow cooker and set on a large plate. Shred chicken with two forks and return to slow cooker. Coarsely break up noodles into soup mixture; add peas and stir gently to mix. Cover and cook for 10 minutes longer or until noodles are tender. Just before serving, stir in onions. Season with pepper, if desired.

Simple Meatless Mexicali Soup

Makes 1 to 2 servings

Ingredients

1 (14 oz.) can chicken broth

2 tsp. taco seasoning, or to taste

1 (3 oz.) pkg. chicken flavor ramen noodles with seasoning packet

Flour tortillas, warmed

Preparation

Pour broth into a medium saucepan over medium heat. Add taco seasoning and stir to dissolve. Heat mixture to boiling. Add noodles and seasoning from packet; cook for 3 minutes or until noodles are tender and flavors are blended. Pour into serving bowls and serve with warm tortillas.

Variation: Add one 11-ounce can mexicorn with red and green bell peppers to soup after noodles are almost tender; cook until heated through.

Slow Cooker Ham Soup

Makes 4 servings

Ingredients

1 (14 oz.) can chicken broth

1 (11.5 oz.) can V-8 juice, regular or spicy hot

1 (15 oz.) can green beans with liquid

1 peeled, diced potato (½" cubes)

⅓ C. chopped ham or pepperoni

1 (3 oz.) pkg. chicken flavor ramen noodles with seasoning packet

Preparation

In a slow cooker, stir together broth, V-8 juice, green beans with liquid, potato, ham and half of the seasoning from packet. Cover and cook on low setting for 3 to 6 hours. About 30 minutes before serving, break up noodles and add to slow cooker with ¾ cup hot water. Stir to combine and continue to cook until noodles are tender and soup is heated through.

Lasagna Soup

Makes about 12 servings

Ingredients

2 tsp. olive oil

1½ lbs. ground Italian sausage

2 onions, finely chopped

4 cloves garlic, minced

2 tsp. oregano

½ tsp. crushed red pepper flakes

2 T. tomato paste

1 (28 oz.) can diced tomatoes with juice

6 C. chicken broth

2 bay leaves

3 (3 oz.) pkgs. ramen noodles, any flavor

½ C. finely chopped fresh basil

Salt and pepper to taste

8 oz. ricotta cheese

½ C. grated Parmesan cheese

¼ tsp. salt

Pinch of pepper

2 C. shredded mozzarella

Preparation

In a large soup pot over medium heat, heat oil. Add sausage and cook until crumbly and no longer pink, about 5 to 7 minutes. Drain any excess fat from pot. Add onion and sauté until softened, about 6 minutes. Add garlic, oregano and red pepper flakes; sauté for 1 minute. Add tomato paste and stir constantly until paste turns a rusty brown, about 5 minutes. Add tomatoes with juice, broth and bay leaves; bring soup to a boil. Reduce heat and simmer for about 30 minutes. Break up noodles and add to soup; discard seasoning packets or reserve for another use. Simmer soup for 3 minutes or until noodles are tender. Discard bay leaves and stir in basil. Season with salt and pepper. Meanwhile in a small bowl, combine ricotta cheese, Parmesan cheese, ¼ teaspoon salt and pinch of pepper; mix well. To serve, spoon approximately 1½ tablespoons of cheese mixture into each serving bowl and sprinkle with some mozzarella cheese. Ladle soup on top.

Beefy Noodle Soup

Makes 8 servings

Ingredients

1 (3 oz.) pkg. beef flavor ramen noodles with seasoning packet

1 lb. lean ground beef

1 (46 oz.) bottle low-sodium V-8 juice

1 (1 oz.) pkg. dry onion soup mix

1 (16 oz.) pkg. frozen mixed vegetables or corn

Preparation

Remove seasoning packet from ramen package and set aside for later use. In a large saucepan over medium heat, brown ground beef, stirring until cooked through and crumbly; drain well. Stir in V-8 juice, soup mix, reserved seasoning from packet and vegetables. Bring mixture to a boil. Reduce heat and simmer, uncovered, for 6 minutes or until vegetables are tender. Return mixture to a boil and coarsely break up noodles into pan. Cook for 3 minutes or until noodles are tender, stirring occasionally. Serve promptly.

Asparagus Soup

Makes 5 to 6 servings

Ingredients

2 tsp. vegetable oil

1 red bell pepper, cored and thinly sliced

1 lb. fresh asparagus, trimmed and cut into 2" pieces

4 oz. sliced deli ham, cut into ½" wide strips

2 (3 oz.) pkgs. chicken flavor ramen noodles with seasoning packets

2 tsp. sesame oil

Preparation

In a large saucepan over high heat, bring 7 cups water to a boil. Meanwhile, heat vegetable oil in a large nonstick skillet over medium-high heat. Add bell pepper and asparagus; cook for 7 minutes or until vegetables are crisp-tender, stirring often. Stir in ham and cook until ham is heated through, about 1 minute; set aside to keep warm. Break up noodles into boiling water; stir in seasoning from both packets. Cook for 3 minutes or until noodles are tender. Remove saucepan from heat; stir in ham mixture and sesame oil. Serve promptly.

Slow-Cooked Thai Chicken Stew

Makes 8 servings

Ingredients

3 medium sweet potatoes, peeled and cubed

2 lbs. boneless, skinless chicken thighs, cubed

1 red bell pepper, cored and thinly sliced

4 C. shredded green cabbage

1 onion, thinly sliced

2 (14 oz.) cans chicken broth

1 (13.5 oz.) can coconut milk

1 tsp. salt

½ tsp. pepper

½ tsp. garlic powder

½ tsp. ground ginger

1 (2.9 oz.) pkg. Thai peanut salad dressing mix

2 (3 oz.) pkgs. ramen noodles, any flavor

Preparation

In a slow cooker, layer in order the sweet potatoes, chicken, bell pepper, cabbage and onion. In a large bowl, whisk together broth, coconut milk, salt, pepper, garlic powder and ginger. Pour broth mixture over layers in slow cooker and cover. Cook on low setting for 7¼ hours; stir once halfway through cooking, if possible. Remove 1½ cups of liquid and discard or reserve for another use. With a ladle, transfer another 1 cup liquid to a small bowl. Add peanut dressing mix and whisk to blend. Pour mixture back into slow cooker. Cover and cook on high setting for 30 minutes. Meanwhile, remove seasoning packets from ramen packages and discard or reserve for another use. Turn off heat, add noodles and cover; let soup stand for 15 minutes or until noodles are tender.

Salads

Chinese Super Slaw

Makes 8 to 10 servings

Ingredients

3 C. shredded green cabbage
1 C. shredded red cabbage
½ C. shredded carrot
5 green onions, sliced
  (about ⅓ C.)
1 (3 oz.) pkg. chicken flavor
  ramen noodles with
  seasoning packet

½ C. vegetable oil
¼ C. white vinegar
1 T. sugar, or more to taste
1 (2 oz.) pkg. slivered
  almonds, toasted*
½ C. sunflower seed kernels
2 tsp. sesame seeds

Preparation

In a large bowl, combine green and red cabbage, carrot and onions. Reserve seasoning packet for use in dressing. Break up noodles and add to cabbage mixture; toss to mix. In a small bowl, whisk together seasoning from packet, oil, vinegar and sugar. Pour dressing over cabbage mixture and toss to coat well. Just before serving, stir in almonds, sunflower kernels and sesame seeds.

* To toast, place almonds in a single layer on a baking sheet. Bake at 350° for approximately 10 minutes or until almonds are golden brown.

Variations: Use a bag of pre-shredded cabbage slaw/cole slaw mix in place of cabbage you shred.

For a sweeter dressing, omit seasoning packet and whisk together ½ cup sugar, ½ cup vegetable oil, ¼ cup cider vinegar and 1 tablespoon soy sauce.

Tossed Lettuce Salad

Makes 4 servings

Ingredients

1 (3 oz.) pkg. chicken flavor
   ramen noodles with
   seasoning packet
4 C. shredded lettuce
1 carrot, grated
4 green onions, sliced
2 T. canola oil

2 T. honey
½ C. rice vinegar
½ C. apple juice
1 (2 oz.) pkg. slivered
   almonds, toasted*
2 T. sesame seeds, toasted*

Preparation

Break up noodles and reserve seasoning packet for use in dressing. In a large bowl, combine lettuce, carrot, onions and uncooked noodles; toss well. In a separate small bowl, whisk together oil, honey, seasoning from packet, vinegar and apple juice until dressing is well blended. Just before serving, sprinkle almonds and sesame seeds on salad and drizzle with desired amount of dressing; toss lightly and serve.

To toast, place almonds in a single layer on a baking sheet. Bake at 350° for 2 to 4 minutes; add sesame seeds and bake for 4 to 6 minutes longer or until almonds and sesame seeds are golden brown.

Variations: *Crumble the noodles into a shallow baking pan and bake at 350° for 5 to 6 minutes or until lightly toasted, stirring occasionally. Cool completely before adding to salad along with sweetened dried cranberries and chopped walnuts.*

For another delicious dressing, whisk together ⅓ cup canola oil, 1 tablespoon brown sugar, 2 tablespoons balsamic vinegar, 2 tablespoons rice wine vinegar, 1 tablespoon soy sauce and the seasoning packet from Oriental flavor ramen noodles.

Ramen Broccoli Slaw

Makes 4 to 6 servings

Ingredients

1 (12 oz.) bag broccoli slaw
4 green onions, sliced
1 C. cashew pieces
1 C. vegetable oil
3 T. rice vinegar

3 T. sugar
Dash of pepper
1 (3 oz.) pkg. Oriental flavor ramen noodles with seasoning packet

Preparation

In a large bowl, combine broccoli slaw, onions and cashews until well mixed; cover and refrigerate for 2 hours or overnight. In a small resealable container, whisk together oil, vinegar, sugar, pepper and the seasoning from packet; seal and refrigerate. Just before serving, break up uncooked noodles into slaw mixture. Pour dressing over salad and toss well to coat.

Italian Ramen Salad

Makes 4 to 6 servings

Ingredients

2 (3 oz.) pkgs. chicken flavor ramen noodles with seasoning packets

2 oz. sliced prosciutto

2 oz. sliced salami

¼ C. quartered artichoke hearts

2 T. olive oil

¼ C. chopped fresh basil

Assorted salad greens

¼ C. crumbled gorgonzola or blue cheese

2 T. pine nuts, toasted*, optional

Preparation

In a medium saucepan over high heat, bring 4 cups water to a boil. Reserve seasoning packets for use in dressing. Break up noodles and add to boiling water; cook for 3 minutes or until tender. Drain well and return to pan. Add prosciutto, salami and artichoke hearts; toss lightly. In a separate bowl, stir together oil, basil and seasoning from reserved packets, mixing well. Pour over noodle mixture and stir gently to coat. Before serving, arrange greens on serving plates and top with ramen salad. Garnish with cheese and pine nuts, if desired.

* To toast, place pine nuts in a single layer on a baking sheet. Bake at 350° for approximately 10 minutes or until pine nuts are golden brown.

Confetti Bean Salad

Makes 4 servings

Ingredients

1 (3 oz.) pkg. chicken flavor ramen noodles with seasoning packet

1⅔ C. canned red, pinto or pink beans, rinsed and drained

½ C. light mayonnaise

¼ C. chopped green bell pepper

¼ C. chopped celery

¼ C. shredded carrot

¼ C. chopped green onions

2 T. diced sweet pickles

2 T. pine nuts, toasted*

Fresh baby spinach leaves

Pickle wedges, optional

Preparation

In a small saucepan over high heat, bring 2 cups water to a boil. Reserve seasoning packet for later use. Break up noodles and add to boiling water; cook for 3 minutes. Drain well, return noodles to pan and cool. In a medium bowl, combine cooled noodles, beans, mayonnaise, bell pepper, celery, carrot, onions, pickles and pine nuts; toss until well blended. Sprinkle seasoning from reserved packet over salad and toss again. Cover and refrigerate for at least 1 hour. To serve, arrange spinach leaves on salad plates and spoon noodle mixture over leaves; garnish with pickle wedges, if desired.

To toast, place pine nuts in a single layer on a baking sheet. Bake at 350° for approximately 10 minutes or until pine nuts are golden brown.

Spinach & Beef Toss

Makes 3 to 4 servings

Ingredients

1 (3 oz.) pkg. Oriental or beef
flavor ramen noodles with
seasoning packet

1 C. fresh spinach
leaves, shredded

½ C. thinly sliced red onion

½ lb. deli roast beef,
sliced into thin strips

2 T. rice vinegar

2 T. canola oil

1 T. prepared horseradish

¼ C. pickled beets,
drained, julienned

1 tsp. poppy seeds

Preparation

In a small saucepan over high heat, bring 2 cups water to a boil.
Reserve seasoning packet for use in dressing. Break up noodles
and add to boiling water; cook for 3 minutes. Drain well and
place noodles in a medium bowl. To noodles, add spinach, onion
and beef; toss to mix well. In a separate bowl, whisk together
vinegar, oil, horseradish and seasoning from reserved packet.
Pour dressing over noodle mixture and toss gently to coat.
Just before serving, top with beets and poppy seeds. Serve
at room temperature.

Crabby Ramen Salad

Makes 4 servings

Ingredients

2 (3 oz.) pkgs. ramen
noodles, any flavor

2 tsp. butter

½ tsp. wasabi paste

Salt and pepper to taste

2 (6 oz.) cans crabmeat

2 T. rice wine vinegar

2 T. sugar

2 T. mayonnaise

1 ripe avocado, seeded,
peeled and diced

1 cucumber, diced

Sesame seeds

Preparation

In a medium saucepan over high heat, bring 4 cups water to
a boil. Remove seasoning packets from ramen packages and
discard or reserve for another use. Break up noodles and add to
boiling water; cook for 3 minutes or until tender. Drain well and
return to pan. While noodles are still warm, stir in butter, wasabi
paste, salt and pepper; mix well. Meanwhile, in a separate bowl,
combine crabmeat, vinegar, sugar and mayonnaise; mix well.
Divide noodles among four serving bowls. Top each serving with
a portion of crabmeat mixture, avocado and cucumber. Garnish
with sesame seeds.

Turkey & Grape Mix

Makes 2 to 4 servings

Ingredients

2 (3 oz.) pkgs. chicken
flavor ramen noodles
with seasoning packets

8 C. baby spinach leaves, torn

1½ C. diced cooked turkey

1 C. red or green grape halves

1 C. slivered red bell pepper

½ C. coarsely
chopped cashews

½ C. crumbled gorgonzola
or blue cheese

4 cloves garlic, minced

Juice from 1 small lemon

⅓ C. olive oil

¼ C. light mayonnaise

Red bell pepper rings, optional

Small grape clusters, optional

Preparation

In a medium saucepan over high heat, bring 4 cups water to a boil. Reserve seasoning packets for use in dressing. Break up noodles and add to boiling water; cook for 3 minutes. Drain well, return noodles to pan and cool. Place cooled noodles in a large bowl. Add spinach, turkey, grape halves, slivered bell pepper, cashews and cheese; toss lightly and set aside. In a small bowl, stir together seasoning from both reserved packets, garlic and lemon juice; let stand for at least 15 minutes. Add oil and mayonnaise and whisk until smooth. Pour dressing over salad and toss until thoroughly mixed. Garnish with bell pepper rings and grape clusters, if desired. Serve immediately.

Citrus Veggie & Noodle Toss

Makes 6 to 8 servings

Ingredients

3 (3 oz.) pkgs. ramen
noodles, any flavor

1½ C. fresh snow peas,
snapped in half

1 yellow summer squash,
cut into thin strips

1 C. shredded carrots

1 C. shredded bok choy
or savoy cabbage

¼ C. orange juice

2 T. honey

4 tsp. white wine vinegar

1 tsp. toasted sesame oil

⅛ tsp. coarse salt

¼ C. olive oil

Orange segments

3 T. toasted sesame seeds*

Preparation

In a large saucepan over high heat, bring 6 cups water to a boil.
Remove seasoning packets from ramen packages and discard
or reserve for another use. Break blocks of noodles in half and
add to boiling water; cook for 3 minutes or until tender, stirring
several times to separate noodles. Drain noodles and rinse under
cold water; drain again. In a large bowl, combine cold noodles,
snow peas, squash, carrots and bok choy; toss well and set aside.
In a small bowl, combine orange juice, honey, vinegar, sesame oil
and salt; whisk vigorously. Slowly whisk in olive oil until blended.
Pour enough dressing over noodle mixture to coat lightly; toss
well. Just before serving, top salad with orange segments and
sesame seeds.

*To toast, place sesame seeds in a single layer on a baking sheet.
 Bake at 350° for approximately 6 to 8 minutes or until sesame
 seeds are brown.*

Peanut Butter & Veggie Salad

Makes 4 servings

Ingredients

2 (3 oz.) pkgs. ramen noodles, any flavor

½ C. creamy peanut butter

¼ C. white vinegar

¼ C. teriyaki sauce

½ tsp. minced garlic

¼ tsp. crushed red pepper flakes, optional

1 cucumber, quartered lengthwise, seeded and sliced

2 carrots, shredded

2 scallions, sliced

Preparation

In a medium saucepan over high heat, bring 4 cups water to a boil. Remove seasoning packets from ramen packages and discard or reserve for another use. Add blocks of noodles to boiling water and cook for 3 minutes or until tender, stirring several times to separate noodles. Drain noodles and rinse under cold water; drain again and set aside. In a medium bowl, combine ¼ cup water, peanut butter, vinegar, teriyaki sauce, garlic and red pepper flakes, if desired. Whisk together until smooth. Add cold noodles, cucumber, carrots and scallions; toss gently to mix. Serve promptly.

Apples 'n Oranges

Makes 4 servings

Ingredients

1 (3 oz.) pkg. ramen noodles, any flavor

2 large oranges

2 Granny Smith apples, or other flavor of choice

4 to 5 T. brown sugar

Preparation

Open the package of noodles and let stand overnight to get stale. Remove seasoning packet and discard or reserve for another use. The next day, peel oranges and separate into segments; cut into bite-size pieces. Core and quarter apples; cut into bite-size pieces. In a medium bowl, toss oranges and apples together. Add brown sugar to taste and toss well. Let stand for at least 20 minutes so juices and sugar form a syrup. Just before serving, break the uncooked noodles into small pieces and mix them into the apples and oranges in bowl.

Fajita Salad

Makes 2 to 4 servings

Ingredients

1 T. chili powder

2 boneless, skinless chicken breast halves

3 T. vegetable oil, divided

1 red or green bell pepper, cored and cut into strips

1 (3 oz.) pkg. picante chicken or chicken ramen noodles with seasoning packet

½ red onion, thinly sliced

¼ C. lime juice

2 T. soy sauce

1 tsp. sugar

2 T. chopped fresh cilantro

Assorted salad greens

Tomato wedges, optional

Avocado wedges, optional

Preparation

Pat chili powder onto both sides of chicken breasts. Heat 1 tablespoon oil in a medium skillet over medium heat. Add chicken and brown both sides; then reduce heat, cover and cook until no longer pink inside. Remove from skillet and cut chicken into strips; transfer to a large bowl. In the same skillet, sauté bell pepper; transfer to bowl with chicken. Break up uncooked noodles and add to bowl along with onion; set aside. In a separate bowl, whisk together seasoning from packet, lime juice, soy sauce, sugar, cilantro and remaining 2 tablespoons oil. Pour dressing over mixture in bowl and toss to coat well. Arrange greens on salad plates and spoon chicken mixture on top. Garnish with tomato and avocado wedges before serving.

Nectarine & Chicken Salad

Makes 4 to 6 servings

Ingredients

¼ C. reduced-sodium chicken broth

3 T. low-sodium soy sauce

2 T. hoisin sauce

1 T. sugar

1 T. salad oil

2 tsp. toasted sesame oil

3 cloves garlic, minced

1½ tsp. grated fresh ginger

1 tsp. crushed red pepper flakes

⅛ tsp. pepper

1 (3 oz.) pkg. ramen noodles, any flavor

¾ lb. diced cooked chicken, kept warm

3 nectarines, plums or peeled peaches, pitted and sliced

2 C. shredded bok choy

¼ C. thinly sliced green onions

Preparation

To make dressing, in a jar with a screw-top lid, combine broth, soy sauce, hoisin sauce, sugar, both oils, garlic, ginger, red pepper flakes and pepper. Cover and shake well to blend; set aside. In a small saucepan over high heat, bring 2 cups water to a boil. Remove seasoning packet from ramen package and discard or reserve for another use. Break up noodles and add to boiling water; cook for 3 minutes or until tender. Drain well. Transfer noodles to a large bowl and drizzle with 3 tablespoons dressing; toss to mix. Divide noodle mixture among four to six serving plates; top each serving with some of the chicken, nectarines, bok choy and onions. Drizzle each salad with some of the remaining dressing.

Fruity Ramen Salad

Makes 3 to 4 servings

Ingredients

1 (3 oz.) pkg. chicken flavor ramen noodles with seasoning packet

3½ T. salad oil, divided

1½ T. lemon juice

1 tsp. sugar

½ C. red or green seedless grape halves

½ C. diced red or green apple

¼ C. diced pineapple

1½ T. chopped fresh chives

4 oz. smoked turkey breast, cut in strips

2 T. chopped walnuts

Preparation

In a small saucepan over high heat, bring 2 cups water to a boil. Reserve seasoning packet for use in dressing. Break up noodles and add to boiling water; cook for 3 minutes or until tender. Drain noodles, rinse with cold water and drain again. In a medium bowl, toss noodles with 1 tablespoon oil, cover and refrigerate for at least 15 minutes. In a small bowl, combine remaining 2½ tablespoons oil, lemon juice, sugar and seasoning from reserved packet; mix well. To cold cooked noodles in bowl, add grapes, apple, pineapple, chives, turkey and walnuts. Pour dressing over mixture in bowl and toss to coat before serving.

Taco Salad

Makes 2 servings

Ingredients

1 (3 oz.) pkg. beef flavor ramen noodles with seasoning packet

½ lb. lean ground beef

1 C. chopped tomato

½ C. chopped onion

Iceberg or romaine lettuce, chopped

1 C. shredded Cheddar cheese

Thousand Island or Western salad dressing to taste

Preparation

In a small saucepan over high heat, bring 2 cups water to a boil. Reserve seasoning packet for later use. Break up noodles and add to boiling water; cook for 3 minutes or until tender. Drain noodles, rinse with cold water and drain again; set aside. Meanwhile, in a small skillet over medium heat, brown ground beef, stirring until cooked through and crumbly. Drain off fat. Stir in half of seasoning from reserved packet, adding 1 to 2 tablespoons water as needed. Cook until heated through. Mix cooked noodles with beef; stir in tomato and onion. Place lettuce in two salad bowls; top each serving with half of beef mixture and cheese. Drizzle with dressing before serving.

Nutty Tofu-Cabbage Slaw

Makes 4 to 6 servings

Ingredients

¼ C. slivered almonds, toasted*

3 T. sesame seeds, toasted*

½ head cabbage, shredded or equivalent bok choy or napa cabbage

1 (3 oz.) pkg. ramen noodles, any flavor

2 T. low-sodium soy sauce

⅓ to ½ C. wine

¼ tsp. garlic powder

¼ tsp. onion powder

¼ tsp. dried cilantro

2 T. sugar

3 T. white vinegar

2 T. sesame oil

2 T. olive oil

4 scallions, thinly sliced

½ C. chopped red bell pepper

2 C. diced extra-firm tofu, drained well

Preparation

In a large bowl, combine almonds, sesame seeds and cabbage. Remove seasoning packet from ramen package and discard or reserve for another use. Break noodles into small pieces and add to bowl; set aside. In a separate bowl, whisk together soy sauce, wine, garlic powder, onion powder, cilantro, sugar, vinegar and both oils. Stir in scallions and bell pepper. Add tofu and marinate for 30 minutes. Pour mixture over cabbage and nuts in bowl; toss gently. Refrigerate for up to 2 hours to blend flavors before serving.

To toast, place almonds in a single layer on a baking sheet. Bake at 350° for 2 to 4 minutes; add sesame seeds and bake for 4 to 6 minutes longer or until almonds and sesame seeds are golden brown.

Zucchini Ramen Blend

Makes 2 servings

Ingredients

1 (3 oz.) pkg. ramen noodles, any flavor
½ C. chopped zucchini
½ C. chopped carrot
2 T. sliced ripe olives

2 T. white vinegar
1 tsp. Dijon mustard
½ tsp. dried basil
¼ tsp. dried oregano
¼ tsp. garlic powder

Preparation

In a small saucepan over high heat, bring 2 cups water to a boil. Remove seasoning packet from ramen package and discard or reserve for another use. Break up noodles and add to boiling water; cook for 3 minutes or until tender. Transfer cooked noodles to a medium bowl. Add zucchini, carrot and olives; toss lightly and set aside. In a small bowl, whisk together vinegar, Dijon mustard, basil, oregano and garlic powder. Pour dressing over noodle mixture and toss to coat well. Serve immediately or chill to serve cold.

Creamy Corn & Peas Salad

Makes 2 servings

Ingredients

1 (3 oz.) pkg. ramen
noodles, any flavor

½ C. frozen corn, thawed

½ C. frozen green
peas, thawed

2 T. minced onion

¼ c. chopped celery, optional

2 to 3 T. mayonnaise,
or more to taste

Salt and pepper, optional

¼ C. cooked,
crumbled bacon

¼ C. shredded Cheddar cheese

Preparation

In a small saucepan over high heat, bring 2 cups water to a boil. Remove seasoning packet from ramen package and discard or reserve for another use. Break up noodles and add to boiling water along with corn; cook for 3 minutes or until noodles are tender. Drain and rinse in cold water; drain again. Place cold cooked noodles and corn in a medium bowl. Add peas, onion and celery, if desired; toss gently. Stir in enough mayonnaise to coat salad ingredients. Season with salt and pepper, if desired. Sprinkle with crumbled bacon and cheese. Serve promptly or chill to serve cold.

Crunchy Cheese & Egg Delight

Makes 2 servings

Ingredients

1 (3 oz.) pkg. shrimp
  flavor ramen noodles
  with seasoning packet

½ C. mayonnaise

1 T. prepared yellow
  mustard, or less to taste

1 T. honey

1 stalk celery,
  coarsely chopped

½ C. cubed mild Cheddar
  or Colby Jack cheese

2 hard-cooked eggs,
  peeled and chopped

Preparation

In a small saucepan over high heat, bring 2 cups water to a boil. Reserve seasoning packet for use in dressing. Break up noodles and add to boiling water; cook for 3 minutes or until tender. Drain and return to pan. Meanwhile, in a medium bowl, stir together mayonnaise, mustard, honey and half the seasoning from reserved packet until well mixed. Add the cooked noodles, celery, cheese and eggs; toss until well coated. Chill before serving.

Simple Antipasto Toss

Makes 4 servings

Ingredients

2 (3 oz.) pkgs. ramen
noodles, any flavor
½ C. sliced pepperoni

½ C. ripe olives
¼ C. sliced Bermuda onion
Italian salad dressing

Preparation

In a medium saucepan over high heat, bring 4 cups water to a boil. Remove seasoning packets from ramen packages and discard or reserve for another use. Break up noodles coarsely and add to boiling water; cook for 3 minutes or until tender. Drain noodles and rinse in cold water; drain again. Place noodles in a medium bowl and add pepperoni, olives and onion. Drizzle with dressing and toss lightly. Serve promptly or chill to serve cold.

Quickie 3-Beaner

Makes 2 to 4 servings

Ingredients

1 (3 oz.) pkg. ramen
noodles, any flavor

½ C. canned green
beans, drained

½ C. kidney beans,
drained and rinsed

½ C. lima beans,
drained and rinsed

¼ C. Italian salad dressing

Preparation

In a small saucepan over high heat, bring 2 cups water to a boil.
Remove seasoning packet from ramen package and discard or
reserve for another use. Break up noodles and add to boiling
water; cook for 3 minutes or until tender. Drain and return to
pan. Add green beans, kidney beans and lima beans and toss
with dressing until coated. Serve promptly.

Spicy Ramen & Vegetable Blend

Makes 4 to 6 servings

Ingredients

3 (3 oz.) pkgs. ramen
noodles, any flavor

5 tsp. vegetable oil, divided

2 oz. fresh snow peas, trimmed
and cut into thin strips

1 carrot, shredded

3 T. minced green
onion and tops

2 T. soy sauce

2 T. creamy peanut butter

2 T. white vinegar

1 T. sugar

1 tsp. minced gingerroot

⅛ to ¼ tsp. cayenne pepper

Preparation

In a large saucepan over high heat, bring 6 cups water to a boil.
Remove seasoning packets from ramen packages and discard
or reserve for another use. Break noodle blocks into fourths and
add to boiling water. Cook for 3 minutes, stirring occasionally;
drain. Rinse with cold water and drain again. Place cold cooked
noodles in a large bowl; toss with 1 teaspoon oil. Place snow
peas in a small bowl and pour 2 cups boiling water over them;
let stand for 30 seconds. Drain and rinse snow peas with cold
water; drain well. Add snow peas, carrot and onion to noodles
in bowl. Cover and refrigerate until chilled. Meanwhile, prepare
dressing in a small bowl by whisking together soy sauce and
peanut butter. Stir in vinegar, remaining 4 teaspoons oil, sugar,
gingerroot and cayenne pepper until well blended. Pour
dressing over noodle mixture and toss to coat well.
Serve immediately.

Crisp Mandarin Orange Slaw

Makes 4 servings

Ingredients

2 (3 oz.) pkgs. chicken flavor ramen noodles with 1 seasoning packet

2 C. shredded cabbage (green or red)

1 C. shredded carrots

4 green onions, chopped

2 T. sesame seeds

½ C. canned mandarin orange segments

2 T. sunflower seed kernels

⅓ C. sugar

⅓ C. light vegetable oil

½ tsp. dry mustard

Salt and pepper to taste

Juice from 1 lime

½ C. pine nuts

½ C. shredded provolone cheese

Preparation

In a medium saucepan over high heat, bring 4 cups water to a boil. Discard one seasoning packet or reserve for another use; set remaining packet aside. Break up noodles and add to boiling water; cook for 3 minutes, stirring occasionally to separate noodles. Drain well; place noodles in a large salad bowl. Add cabbage, carrots, onions, sesame seeds, oranges and sunflower kernels; toss well. In a small bowl, whisk together sugar, oil, dry mustard, salt, pepper, lime juice and seasoning from one packet. Drizzle over noodle mixture. Just before serving, sprinkle with pine nuts and cheese.

Ramen Tuna Salad

Makes 4 servings

Ingredients

2 (3 oz.) pkgs. chicken
flavor ramen noodles
with seasoning packet(s)

1 head cabbage, shredded

2 (5 oz.) cans tuna in
water, drained

¼ C. sliced almonds

¼ C. sunflower seed kernels

½ C. vegetable oil

5 T. white vinegar

5 T. rice vinegar

Preparation

Break up uncooked noodles into a large bowl; reserve seasoning
packets for use in dressing. To noodles, add cabbage, tuna,
almonds and sunflower kernels; toss until well mixed and set
aside. In a small bowl, whisk together oil, both vinegars and
seasoning from one or both packets, according to taste. Pour
dressing over cabbage mixture and stir to combine. Chill for
several hours. Toss again before serving.

Greek Salad

Makes 4 to 6 servings

Ingredients

2 (3 oz.) pkgs. ramen
noodles, any flavor

1 C. chopped red bell pepper

½ C. chopped onion

½ C. sliced ripe olives

½ C. sliced green olives

½ C. chopped tomato

1 C. cubed feta cheese

½ C. canola oil

¼ C. orange or lemon juice

Salt and pepper to taste

Preparation

In a medium saucepan over high heat, bring 4 cups water
to a boil. Remove seasoning packets from ramen packages
and discard or reserve for another use. Add blocks of noodles
to boiling water; cook for 3 minutes or until tender, stirring
frequently to separate noodles. Drain well and transfer noodles
to a medium serving bowl. Arrange bell pepper, onion, ripe
olives, green olives, tomato and cheese on top of noodles. In a
small bowl, stir together oil and orange juice; season with salt
and pepper. Drizzle dressing over salad in bowl and serve.

Chilled Japanese Noodle Salad

Makes 2 servings

Ingredients

3 T. soy sauce
2 T. sugar
3 T. white vinegar
5 T. chicken stock or broth
1 tsp. sesame oil
½ tsp. chili oil, optional
2 (3 oz.) pkgs. ramen
  noodles, any flavor

1 egg, beaten
½ cucumber, julienned
1 carrot, grated
1 slice cooked ham,
  cut into thin strips
¼ sheet nori, crumbled
1 T. hot Chinese
  mustard, optional

Preparation

In a small bowl, stir together soy sauce, sugar, vinegar, chicken stock, sesame oil and chili oil, if desired, until sugar dissolves; set dressing aside. In a medium saucepan over high heat, bring 4 cups water to a boil. Remove seasoning packets from ramen packages and discard or reserve for another use. Add noodles to boiling water and cook for 2 minutes, stirring occasionally to separate noodles. Drain and refrigerate noodles until cold. Meanwhile, coat a small nonstick skillet with nonstick cooking spray and place over medium heat. Add egg and tilt pan to thinly coat bottom with egg. When firm, fold the egg in half and remove from pan; slice into thin strips. To serve, place cold noodles on serving plates. Top each with part of the egg, cucumber, carrot and ham. Pour dressing over the top and sprinkle with crumbled nori. Serve with hot mustard on the side.

Variations: *Replace the ham with thinly sliced pork, shrimp, chicken or turkey. Whisk the mustard into the sauce and eat warm.*

Poppy Seed Spring Salad

Makes 12 servings

Ingredients

1 (3 oz.) pkg. ramen
noodles, any flavor

1 (5 oz.) pkg. spring mix
salad greens

½ head iceberg lettuce, torn

1 (11 oz.) can mandarin
oranges, drained

¼ C. slivered
almonds, toasted*

3 T. cider vinegar

6 T. sugar

½ small white or red
onion, cut into wedges

¼ tsp. salt

¼ tsp. dry mustard

½ C. canola oil

2 tsp. poppy seeds

Preparation

Remove seasoning packet from ramen package and discard or reserve for another use. Break up uncooked noodles into a large bowl. Add salad greens, lettuce, oranges and almonds; toss well and set aside. To make dressing, in a blender container, combine vinegar, sugar, onion, salt and dry mustard; cover and process until smooth. While processing, gradually add oil in a steady stream. Stir in poppy seeds. Serve dressing with salad.

* To toast, place almonds in a single layer on a baking sheet.
  Bake at 350° for approximately 10 minutes or until almonds
  are golden brown.

Main Dishes

Breakfast Burritos

Makes 2 servings

Ingredients

1 (3 oz.) pkg. ramen noodles with seasoning packet, flavor of choice

2 eggs, lightly beaten

½ C. shredded Colby-Jack or Cheddar cheese

Hot pepper sauce

2 flour tortillas, warmed

Preparation

In a small saucepan over high heat, bring 2 cups water to a boil. Reserve seasoning packet for later use; break up noodles and add to boiling water. Slowly pour beaten eggs into water with noodles; stir and cook for 3 minutes. Drain off all but about 1 tablespoon water. Stir in seasoning from reserved packet, cheese and pepper sauce to taste. Divide mixture between warm tortillas and roll up or wrap as desired. Serve immediately.

Ham & Cheesy Noodle Frittata

Makes 3 to 4 servings

Ingredients

2 (3 oz.) pkgs. chicken
    flavor ramen noodles
    with 1 seasoning packet
6 eggs
2 tsp. butter

4 thin slices deli-style
    ham, diced
¼ C. sliced green onions
½ C. shredded Cheddar cheese

Preparation

Preheat oven to 400°. Set aside one seasoning packet and discard remaining packet or reserve for another use. In a medium saucepan over high heat, bring 4 cups water to a boil. Add blocks of noodles to boiling water and cook for 3 minutes or until tender, stirring occasionally to separate noodles; drain well. In a medium bowl, whisk together eggs and one packet of seasoning. Stir in cooked noodles and set aside. In a large oven-proof skillet over medium-high heat, melt butter. Add ham and onion, and cook until tender, about 3 minutes. Shake skillet to distribute ham and onions evenly; add egg mixture and sprinkle top with cheese. Transfer skillet to oven and bake for 6 to 8 minutes or until eggs are set and cheese melts. Cut into wedges and serve.

Variation: *To make Cheesy Noodle Frittata, simply omit ham and serve wedges with salsa.*

Mexican Frittata

Makes 12 servings

Ingredients

2 (3 oz.) pkgs. beef flavor ramen noodles with seasoning packets

1 (15.25 oz.) can whole kernel corn, drained

1 (4.5 oz.) can chopped green chilies, undrained

3 green onions, sliced

¼ tsp. crushed red pepper flakes

3 Roma tomatoes, chopped

1 C. shredded Colby-Jack cheese

3 eggs

1½ C. milk

8 ripe olives, sliced

Salsa, optional

Sour cream, optional

Preparation

Preheat oven to 350°. Lightly coat a 9 x 13″ baking dish with nonstick cooking spray; set aside. In a large saucepan over high heat, bring 4 cups water to a boil. Reserve seasoning packets for later use. Break up noodles and add to boiling water. Cook noodles for 3 minutes; drain well. Spread cooked noodles in the bottom of prepared baking dish. Sprinkle the seasoning from one (or both) reserved packets evenly over noodles. Layer corn, chilies, green onions, red pepper flakes, tomatoes and cheese over noodles in order given. In a medium bowl, beat eggs with milk. Pour egg mixture over layers in dish. Top with olives. Bake for 30 to 33 minutes or until lightly browned and set. Let stand several minutes before cutting into squares. Serve with salsa and sour cream, if desired.

Goulash with a Kick

Makes 3 to 4 servings

Ingredients

½ lb. lean ground beef
1 (5.5 oz.) can low-sodium
   V-8 juice

2 (3 oz.) pkgs. chili flavor
   ramen noodles with
   1 seasoning packet
1½ C. frozen mixed vegetables

Preparation

In a large skillet over medium heat, brown ground beef, stirring until cooked through and crumbly; remove from skillet and drain well. To same skillet, add 1¼ cups water, V-8 juice and seasoning from one packet; discard remaining packet or reserve for another use. Stir mixture well and bring to a boil. Add vegetables and cook for 3 minutes. Lightly break up noodles and add to skillet; stir to mix well and cook for 2 minutes. Return cooked, drained beef to skillet. Cover, reduce heat to medium-low and simmer for 3 to 4 minutes or until noodles are tender and most of the liquid has been absorbed. Uncover and simmer 1 to 2 minutes longer to desired consistency. Serve promptly.

Ramen Shepherd's Pie

Makes 4 servings

Ingredients

1 lb. lean ground beef

1 C. chopped onion

1 to 2 cloves garlic, minced

2 C. frozen green peas
and carrots or corn

2 (3 oz.) pkgs. beef flavor
ramen noodles with
1 seasoning packet

Preparation

Preheat oven to 350°. In a medium skillet over medium heat, cook ground beef, onion and garlic until beef is browned and crumbly and onions are tender. Drain well and set aside. Meanwhile, in a medium saucepan over high heat, bring 3 cups water to a boil. Stir in seasoning from one packet; discard remaining packet or reserve for another use. Break up noodles and add to boiling water. Cook for 3 minutes, stirring occasionally; drain well. Transfer beef mixture to a glass baking dish. Sprinkle peas and carrots over the meat. Arrange cooked noodles over the top and bake for 10 to 15 minutes or until heated through.

Herbed Skillet Chicken

Makes 2 servings

Ingredients

1 (3 oz.) pkg. chicken flavor ramen noodles with seasoning packet

2 T. butter

1 boneless, skinless chicken breast half, diced

½ C. chopped onion

2 T. flour

1 T. vinegar

1 T. snipped fresh parsley

½ to 1 tsp. dried tarragon

½ to 1 tsp. dried thyme

Preparation

Reserve seasoning packet for later use. In a small skillet over medium heat, melt butter. Add chicken and sauté until chicken is cooked through, stirring often. Stir in onion and flour; cook until deep brown. Meanwhile, in a small saucepan, bring 2 cups water to a boil. Break up noodles and add to boiling water. Cook for 3 minutes or until tender, stirring occasionally. Drain noodles and return to pan to keep warm. To the chicken in the skillet, add 1 cup water, vinegar, parsley, tarragon, thyme and half of the seasoning from reserved packet. Bring to a boil, reduce heat and simmer for 1 minute. Serve chicken mixture over hot noodles.

Noodled Chicken Parmesan

Makes 2 servings

Ingredients

2 boneless, skinless chicken
   breast halves

2 T. milk

⅓ C. finely crushed
   bread crumbs

2 T. olive oil

2 C. spaghetti sauce

1 C. grated Parmesan cheese

2 (3 oz.) pkgs. ramen
   noodles, any flavor

Preparation

Dip chicken into milk and roll in bread crumbs to coat well. In a medium skillet over medium-high heat, heat oil. Add chicken and cook until golden brown and cooked through, turning once halfway through cooking time; drain. Reduce heat and add spaghetti sauce to pan; simmer until heated through. Sprinkle cheese over the chicken; continue cooking until cheese is melted, about 2 minutes. Meanwhile, in a small saucepan, bring 2 cups water to a boil. Remove seasoning packets from ramen packages and discard or reserve for another use. Break up noodles and add to boiling water; cook for 3 minutes, stirring occasionally. Drain well. Serve chicken and sauce over hot noodles.

Tex-Mex Ramen

Makes 4 servings

Ingredients

1 lb. lean ground beef
1 (1 oz.) env. taco seasoning
1 (3 oz.) pkg. beef flavor ramen noodles with seasoning packet
1 C. diced tomato
½ C. chopped onion

1 C. shredded Mexican blend cheese
Chopped fresh cilantro
2 C. coarsely crushed nacho cheese tortilla chips
Salsa, optional
Sour cream, optional

Preparation

In a medium skillet over medium heat, brown ground beef, stirring until cooked through and crumbly; drain well. Reduce heat and add taco seasoning and ⅓ cup water; stir well while simmering for several minutes. Meanwhile, in a small saucepan over high heat, bring 2 cups water to a boil; stir in seasoning from packet. Add noodles and cook for 3 minutes, stirring occasionally; drain well. Add cooked noodles to meat mixture and toss to blend. Place on serving plates and top with some of the tomato, onion, cheese, cilantro and tortilla chips. Serve with salsa and sour cream, if desired.

Quick Hamburger Nachos

Makes 4 servings

Ingredients

2 (3 oz.) pkgs. beef flavor
   ramen noodles with
   seasoning packets
1 lb. lean ground beef
1 (10 oz.) bag nacho
   cheese tortilla chips,
   coarsely broken

2 C. shredded Cheddar cheese
Sour cream, optional
Chopped tomatoes, optional
Chopped onion, optional

Preparation

In a medium saucepan over high heat, bring 4 cups water to
a boil. Add seasoning from one packet; break up noodles and
add to boiling water. Cook for 3 minutes or until tender. Drain
noodles and return to pan; set aside. Meanwhile, in a medium
skillet over medium heat, brown ground beef with seasoning
from second packet, stirring until cooked through and crumbly.
Add beef mixture to cooked noodles and mix well. On each
serving plate, arrange a bed of tortilla chips. Place some of the
beef mixture on top of chips and sprinkle with cheese. Garnish
with sour cream, tomatoes and onion, if desired.

Simple Thai Chicken

Makes 2 servings

Ingredients

1 (3 oz.) pkg. ramen
noodles, any flavor

2 T. soy sauce

2 T. creamy peanut butter

1 tsp. garlic powder

1 tsp. chili powder

1 C. hot diced cooked chicken

4 green onions, sliced

Preparation

Remove seasoning packet from ramen package and discard or reserve for another use. In a small saucepan over high heat, bring 2 cups water to a boil. Break up noodles and add to boiling water. Cook for 3 minutes, stirring occasionally; drain noodles and return to pan. Meanwhile, in a small bowl, whisk together soy sauce, peanut butter, garlic powder and chili powder. Stir peanut butter mixture into hot noodles with chicken; sprinkle with onions and serve immediately.

Oriental Shrimp & Vegetables

Makes 4 servings

Ingredients

1 (14 to 16 oz.) pkg. medium to large frozen shrimp, thawed*

1 (3 oz.) pkg. Oriental flavor ramen noodles with seasoning packet

1 (16 oz.) pkg. frozen stir-fry vegetables, any type

¼ C. stir-fry sauce

Preparation

Heat a large nonstick skillet over medium-high heat. Add shrimp and cook for 2 to 4 minutes, stirring frequently, until pink and firm. Remove shrimp from skillet and keep warm. In the same skillet, heat 2 cups water to boiling. Break up noodles slightly and add to water; reserve seasoning packet. Cook noodles for 1 to 2 minutes, until slightly softened. Stir in vegetables. Bring to a boil and cook mixture for 3 to 6 minutes, stirring occasionally, until vegetables are crisp-tender. Stir in seasoning from reserved packet. Add stir-fry sauce and cook 3 to 4 minutes longer or until just heated through, stirring frequently. Stir in shrimp and serve promptly.

Variation: *Use 1 pound of thinly sliced beef strips in place of shrimp; spray skillet with nonstick cooking spray and cook beef for 3 to 5 minutes or until brown. Then proceed as directed.*

* Fresh uncooked, peeled and deveined shrimp may also be used.

Ballpark Ramen

Makes 2 to 4 servings

Ingredients

½ lb. kielbasa or other smoked sausage

1 (14.5 oz.) can sauerkraut

½ C. chopped onion

¼ C. chopped green or yellow bell pepper

1 tsp. brown sugar

¼ tsp. caraway seed, optional

Salt and pepper to taste

2 (3 oz.) pkgs. beef flavor ramen noodles

¼ C. sweet pickle relish, optional

Sliced jalapeño peppers, optional

Preparation

Preheat a grill to medium heat. Place sausage on grill and cook until heated through and browned on outside, turning several times. In a medium saucepan over medium-low heat, combine sauerkraut, onion, bell pepper, brown sugar and caraway seed, if desired; bring to a simmer, stirring occasionally. When sausage is done, slice and add to saucepan. Season with salt and pepper; simmer for 4 to 5 minutes, stirring several times. Meanwhile, in a small saucepan over high heat, bring 2 cups water to a boil. Remove seasoning packet from ramen package and discard or reserve for another use. Break up noodles and add to boiling water; cook noodles for 3 minutes or until tender. Drain and divide noodles between serving bowls. Top each serving with a portion of sauerkraut and sausage mixture and garnish with pickle relish and jalapeños, if desired.

Ham & Veggie Fritters

Makes 4 servings

Ingredients

2 (3 oz.) pkgs. pork flavor
   ramen noodles with
   seasoning packets
3 slices ham, diced
¼ C. grated carrot
¼ C. grated zucchini
⅓ C. grated Parmesan cheese

2 T. diced green
   onions, optional
Salt and pepper to taste
4 eggs, lightly beaten
Sour cream, optional
Salsa, optional

Preparation

In a medium saucepan over high heat, bring 4 cups water to a
boil. Coarsely crush noodles and add to boiling water; reserve
seasoning packets. Cook noodles for 3 minutes or until tender;
drain and return to pan. Add seasoning from both reserved
packets and stir gently to coat noodles. Stir in ham, carrot,
zucchini, cheese and onions; season with salt and pepper. Let
mixture cool slightly and then stir in eggs until well combined.
Coat a medium nonstick skillet with nonstick cooking spray and
place over medium heat. When hot, pour ¼ cup of egg mixture
into skillet and fry for about 2 minutes per side. Repeat with
remaining mixture. Serve with sour cream and salsa, if desired.

Slow Cooker Beef & Noodles

Makes 8 to 12 servings

Ingredients

1 (2 to 3 lb.) boneless
beef roast

6 to 10 (3 oz.) pkgs. beef
flavor ramen noodles with
seasoning packets

Preparation

Trim any excess fat from the roast. Place roast in a slow cooker
on low setting and add 1 cup water. Cover and cook for 8 hours
or overnight. Remove roast and shred the meat with two forks;
return meat to slow cooker. Remove the seasoning packets from
6 to 10 packages of ramen noodles, depending on how many
people you wish to serve. To the meat in the slow cooker, add
½ cup water and the seasoning from opened packages of
noodles, or to taste; stir to blend. Cover slow cooker and
continue to cook on low setting for 6 to 8 hours. One hour
before serving, bring a large pot of water to a boil over high
heat. Add noodles from opened packages and cook until almost
tender, about 3 minutes. Drain and add cooked noodles to slow
cooker with beef. Add ½ cup water and stir together gently
until combined. Cook for 30 minutes longer to blend flavors.

Ramen Pizza

Makes 8 servings

Ingredients

2 (3 oz.) pkgs. beef flavor
ramen noodles with
seasoning packets

½ lb. lean ground beef

½ C. chopped onion

½ C. sliced mushrooms

1 egg

½ C. milk

3 T. grated Parmesan cheese

1 (14 to 15 oz.) can or
jar pizza sauce

2 C. shredded
mozzarella cheese

Preparation

Preheat oven to 350°. Cover a 12″ pizza pan with aluminum foil.
Build up edges to form a ½″ tall rim around the pan. Coat foil
with nonstick cooking spray; set aside. In a medium saucepan
over high heat, bring 4 cups water to a boil. Break up noodles
and add to boiling water; reserve seasoning packets for later
use. Cook noodles for 3 minutes or until tender; drain and set
aside. In a medium skillet over medium heat, combine ground
beef, onion and mushrooms; cook, stirring often, until beef is
browned and crumbly and onions are tender. Drain excess fat.
Stir seasoning from both reserved packets into meat mixture;
set aside. In a small bowl, beat together egg, milk and Parmesan
cheese. Pour egg mixture into noodles and stir well. Spread
noodle mixture onto prepared pizza pan and shape to form the
crust. Spread pizza sauce over noodles. Sprinkle meat mixture
over sauce and top with mozzarella cheese. Bake for 20 minutes
or until golden brown and bubbly. Let stand 5 minutes before
slicing into wedges.

Tuna Noodle Casserole

Makes 4 servings

Ingredients

1 (3 oz.) pkg. ramen
noodles, any flavor
¼ C. butter
1 C. chopped celery
¼ C. chopped onion
¼ C. flour
2 T. Dijon mustard
¼ tsp. pepper

2¼ C. milk
1 (12 oz.) can chunk
tuna, drained
½ C. chopped roasted
red pepper
½ C. crushed potato
chips or whole
wheat crackers

Preparation

Preheat oven to 375°. Coat a 1½-quart baking dish with nonstick cooking spray; set aside. Remove seasoning packet from ramen package and discard or reserve for another use. In a large saucepan over high heat, bring 2 cups water to a boil. Break up noodles and add to boiling water; cook for 3 minutes or until tender. Drain noodles and return to pan; set aside. In a medium saucepan over medium heat, melt butter. Add celery and onion; sauté until almost tender. Stir in flour, Dijon mustard and pepper until bubbly. Add milk and cook while whisking until slightly thickened, smooth and bubbly. Add sauce, tuna and red pepper to noodles, folding in gently until combined. Transfer to prepared baking dish. Sprinkle potato chips on top. Bake uncovered for 30 to 35 minutes. Let stand 5 minutes before serving.

Variations: Add 1 cup mixed vegetables and 1 cup shredded mozzarella cheese to mixture before baking.

Use hot and spicy chicken flavor ramen noodles with 1 cup Asian style stir-fry vegetables and the seasoning packet in place of the mustard and pepper in recipe.

Quick Sesame Chicken

Makes 6 servings

Ingredients

⅓ C. rice vinegar

⅓ C. thinly sliced green onions

2 T. honey

1 T. low-sodium soy sauce

1 T. grated fresh ginger

2 tsp. Asian garlic-chili sauce

2 (6 oz.) pkgs. refrigerated grilled chicken breast strips*

3 (3 oz.) pkgs. ramen noodles, any flavor

3 T. toasted sesame oil

2 bell peppers, cored and cut into strips (yellow, red, green or orange)

Fresh cilantro

Preparation

In a medium bowl, whisk together vinegar, onions, honey, soy sauce, ginger and garlic-chili sauce. Add chicken and toss until coated. Allow mixture to stand for 10 minutes for flavors to blend. Meanwhile, remove seasoning packets from ramen packages and discard or reserve for another use. In a large saucepan over high heat, bring 6 cups water to a boil. Break up noodles and add to boiling water; cook for 3 to 4 minutes or until tender. Drain noodles and return to pan. Drizzle noodles with oil and toss to coat. Add chicken mixture and stir gently to combine. Transfer to serving bowls and top each with bell pepper strips and cilantro.

Grill your own chicken breasts and cut into thin strips or use leftovers to make this dish.

Broccoli & Chicken Casserole

Makes 4 servings

Ingredients

2 C. frozen broccoli,
slightly thawed

2 (3 oz.) pkgs. chicken flavor
ramen noodles with
seasoning packets

1 T. butter

½ C. French onion dip
or plain sour cream

¾ C. Velveeta chunks

Salt and pepper to taste

½ C. butter cracker
crumbs (such as Ritz)

Preparation

Preheat oven to 350°. Lightly coat a medium casserole dish with
nonstick cooking spray; set aside. In a medium saucepan over
high heat, bring 4 cups water to a boil. Add broccoli and cook for
2 minutes. Break up noodles and add to boiling water; reserve
seasoning packets for later use. Cook noodles for 3 minutes more
or until tender. Drain most of water, leaving 1 to 2 tablespoons
in pan. Add butter and onion dip; sprinkle seasoning from
both packets over the top and stir until blended. Stir in cheese
and season with salt and pepper. Transfer noodle mixture to
prepared baking dish and bake for 15 minutes. Remove from
oven and sprinkle cracker crumbs on top; return to oven to
bake for 6 minutes longer or until crumbs are golden brown.

Mock Egg Fu Yung

Makes 4 servings

Ingredients

3 T. vegetable oil

1 C. chopped celery

1 C. chopped green onions

1 C. frozen small shrimp, thawed and chopped

3 T. soy sauce

¼ tsp. fresh grated ginger, or to taste

1 (3 oz.) pkg. shrimp flavor ramen noodles with seasoning packet

3 eggs

Additional oil for frying

Prepared brown gravy, optional

Fresh parsley, optional

Preparation

In a medium saucepan over medium heat, heat oil. Add celery, onions and shrimp; sauté until vegetables are crisp-tender. Stir in soy sauce and ginger; set aside to cool. In a small saucepan over high heat, bring 1¼ cups water to a boil. Break up noodles and add to boiling water along with seasoning from packet. Cook noodles for 3 minutes or until tender. Meanwhile, in a small bowl, beat eggs until pale yellow; set aside. When noodles are cooked, drain off excess liquid; add sautéed mixture with liquid and stir gently to coat. Add beaten egg. In a clean skillet over medium-high heat, pour 1⁄16″ oil. When hot, spoon egg mixture into pan to make 4″ omelets. Fry until golden brown, turning partway through cooking time. To serve omelets, drizzle with gravy and garnish with parsley, if desired.

Skillet Tofu

Makes 1 to 2 servings

Ingredients

1 (3.55 oz.) pkg. Sapporo Ichiban miso flavor ramen noodles with seasoning packet

1 T. sesame oil

⅓ block firm or extra-firm tofu, drained and cut into small pieces

1 to 2 green onions, chopped

Cayenne pepper, optional

Preparation

Reserve seasoning packet for later use. In a small saucepan, bring 2 cups water to a boil. Add noodles and cook for 3 minutes or until tender. Meanwhile, in a small skillet over medium-high heat, heat oil. Add tofu and fry for 2 minutes, stirring constantly. Add onions and fry for 1 minute while stirring. Reduce heat to medium. When noodles are tender, drain off most of the water, leaving about ⅓ cup water in pan with noodles. Add seasoning from packet and stir until dissolved. Transfer noodles to skillet with tofu. Cook and stir for 2 minutes or until water is absorbed. Season with cayenne pepper, if desired.

Chicken Noodle Strudel

Makes 4 servings

Ingredients

2 (3 oz.) pkgs. chicken flavor ramen noodles with seasoning packets

1 egg, beaten

1 tsp. sesame oil

2 C. thinly sliced boneless, skinless chicken breast

1 C. chopped red bell pepper

1 C. broccoli florets

1 (8 oz.) can crushed pineapple in syrup

1 T. sugar

1 T. vinegar

2 tsp. cornstarch

Additional broccoli and red bell pepper, optional

Preparation

Coat a 9″ to 10″ deep-dish pie pan with nonstick cooking spray; set aside. Preheat oven to 350°. In a medium saucepan over high heat, bring 4 cups water to a boil. Reserve seasoning packets for later use. Break up noodles and add to boiling water; cook for 3 minutes or until tender. Drain well and return to saucepan. Stir in egg. Place half of noodle mixture into bottom of pie pan; set aside. Meanwhile, heat oil in a medium saucepan over medium heat. Add chicken and sauté for approximately 5 minutes, stirring frequently. Add bell pepper and broccoli; sauté for 3 minutes more. Stir in seasoning from reserved packets, pineapple with syrup, sugar, vinegar and cornstarch. Cook for 3 to 5 minutes or until thickened. Place chicken mixture over noodles in pie pan. Top with remaining noodles. Bake for 20 minutes. Garnish with broccoli and bell pepper, if desired. Cut into wedges to serve.

Stovetop Salmon & Vegetable Toss

Makes 4 servings

Ingredients

2 (3 oz.) pkgs. Oriental
   flavor ramen noodles
   with seasoning packets
1 T. butter
1 C. finely chopped onion
1½ C. milk

4 oz. cream cheese, cubed
1 C. julienned carrots
1 C. julienned zucchini
2 (6.5 to 7.5 oz.) cans salmon,
   drained and flaked, bones
   removed as needed

Preparation

Reserve seasoning packets for later use. In a medium skillet
over medium heat, melt butter. Add onion and sauté for
2 minutes. Add milk, cream cheese and seasoning from one
reserved packet; cook and stir until mixture is hot and smooth,
but do not boil. Add carrots, zucchini and salmon; simmer for
5 minutes. Meanwhile, in a medium saucepan over high heat,
bring 4 cups water to a boil. Break up noodles and add to
boiling water with the seasoning from remaining packet;
cook for 3 minutes or until tender; drain well. Add cooked
noodles to salmon mixture and toss gently until blended.
Serve immediately.

Turkey Lo Mein

Makes 4 servings

Ingredients

2 T. vegetable oil

¾ lb. turkey or chicken tenders, thinly sliced

2 (3 oz.) pkgs. ramen noodles, any flavor

⅓ C. creamy peanut butter

¼ tsp. crushed red pepper flakes

2 T. soy sauce

1 T. dark sesame oil

1 (15 oz.) can straw mushrooms, drained

1 (16 oz.) pkg. frozen stir-fry vegetables (broccoli, carrots, water chestnuts and red bell pepper)

Preparation

Heat vegetable oil in a medium nonstick skillet over medium heat. Add turkey and cook until browned on both sides and no longer pink inside, about 5 minutes; set aside and keep warm. In a 3-quart microwave-safe casserole dish, heat 2 cups water on high power for 3 minutes. Remove seasoning packets from ramen packages and discard or reserve for another use. Separate noodles into layers and arrange in casserole dish so that all noodles are in the water. Cover with plastic wrap, turning back one corner to vent. Cook on high power for 5 minutes, stirring once partway through cooking time to separate noodles. Meanwhile, in a small bowl, whisk together ½ cup hot water, peanut butter, red pepper flakes, soy sauce and sesame oil until blended. To noodles, add peanut butter mixture, mushrooms, vegetables and turkey strips; mix well. Cover and vent. Cook on high power for 5 minutes or until vegetables are crisp-tender, stirring once.

Italian Skillet

Makes 4 servings

Ingredients

2 (3 oz.) pkgs. beef flavor
ramen noodles with
1 seasoning packet

1 lb. lean ground beef

24 slices pepperoni

1 (14.5 oz.) can diced
tomatoes with basil, garlic
and oregano, with juice

½ C. diced green bell pepper

1 C. shredded
mozzarella cheese

Preparation

Discard one seasoning packet or reserve for another use; set
aside remaining packet. Break noodles in half; set aside. In a
large skillet over medium heat, cook ground beef and pepperoni
for 8 to 10 minutes, stirring occasionally, until beef is browned
and crumbly. Drain off fat. Stir in 1 cup water, tomatoes with juice
and seasoning from one packet; heat to boiling. Add uncooked
noodles and bell pepper; cook for 3 to 5 minutes or until noodles
are tender, stirring occasionally. Sprinkle cheese on noodle
mixture in a ring around the edge of skillet. Cover and let stand
about 5 minutes or until cheese melts.

Gourmet Tuna Bake

Makes 4 to 6 servings

Ingredients

½ C. butter, divided

1 C. chopped onion, divided

1½ C. stuffing mix
or crushed crackers

2 to 3 T. white wine

1 C. milk

1 C. chicken broth

1 T. dry mustard

3 dashes of pepper

1 C. shredded Cheddar cheese

4 slices American cheese

2 (3 oz.) pkgs. ramen
noodles, any flavor

2 (5 oz.) cans tuna,
drained and flaked

Preparation

Preheat oven to 375°. Lightly coat a medium casserole dish with nonstick cooking spray; set aside. In a medium skillet over low heat, melt 6 tablespoons butter. Add ¾ cup onion and sauté until softened, about 2 minutes. Add stuffing mix and stir to coat mixture well. Add wine, mix well and cover pan. Cook for 4 minutes, stirring occasionally, and then set aside. Meanwhile, in a medium saucepan over medium-low heat, combine milk, broth, remaining 2 tablespoons butter, dry mustard and pepper; cook until hot, but not boiling. Reduce heat to low and add Cheddar and American cheeses and remaining ¼ cup onion. Continue to cook until cheese melts. Remove seasoning packets from ramen packages and discard or reserve for another use. Break noodles into four pieces and add to milk mixture. Cook until noodles are soft and separated. Add tuna and mix well. Pour mixture into prepared casserole dish and top with stuffing mixture. Bake for 30 minutes.

Pork Lo Mein

Makes 4 servings

Ingredients

2 (3 oz.) pkgs. Oriental
flavor ramen noodles
with seasoning packets

2 tsp. olive oil, divided

1 onion, sliced

3 cloves garlic, minced

1 (16 oz.) bag frozen stir-fry
vegetables, any type, thawed

12 oz. pork cutlets or
boneless thin-cut pork
chops, cut into strips

1 T. cornstarch

Sliced scallions, optional

Preparation

Reserve seasoning packets for later use. In a medium saucepan over high heat, bring 4 cups water to a boil. Break up noodles and add to boiling water; cover pan and turn off heat. Allow noodles to stand for 5 minutes or until tender. Drain and set aside. Meanwhile, in a large nonstick skillet over medium heat, heat 1 teaspoon oil. Add onion and sauté for 5 minutes or until tender, stirring often. Add garlic and cook for 1 minute or until fragrant. Add vegetables. Stir-fry for 3 minutes or until crisp-tender; transfer mixture to a bowl. In the same skillet, heat remaining 1 teaspoon oil. Add pork, in two batches if necessary. Stir-fry for 2 minutes or until browned and cooked through; transfer meat to bowl with vegetables. In the same skillet, whisk together 1 cup water, the seasoning from one (or both) packets and cornstarch. Bring to a simmer, stirring constantly. Cook for 1 minute or until slightly thickened. Add cooked noodles, vegetables and pork; toss to coat well. Cook over low heat, stirring gently until warmed through.

Pineapple Meatballs & Noodles

Makes 4 servings

Ingredients

½ lb. lean ground beef
2 to 3 T. Worcestershire sauce
1 tsp. garlic powder
1 tsp. salt, optional
⅓ C. vegetable oil

2 (3 oz.) pkgs. ramen noodles, any flavor
½ C. pineapple chunks
½ C. chopped red bell pepper

Preparation

In a medium bowl, combine ground beef, Worcestershire sauce, garlic powder and salt, if desired. Mix well, using hands as needed. Shape meat mixture into small balls. Place oil in a medium skillet over medium heat. When hot, add meatballs and cook until evenly browned, turning frequently. Reduce heat and simmer for 10 minutes. Meanwhile, remove seasoning packets from ramen packages and discard or reserve for another use. In a medium saucepan over high heat, bring 4 cups water to a boil. Break up noodles slightly and add to boiling water; cook for 3 minutes or until noodles are tender. Drain noodles and return to pan; set aside and keep warm. When meatballs are cooked through, add pineapple and bell pepper to skillet; cook for 5 minutes or until heated through and crisp-tender. To serve, place cooked noodles on a serving platter and top with meatballs and vegetable mixture.

Chicken Hollandaise

Makes 2 servings

Ingredients

1 (3 oz.) pkg. chicken
flavor ramen noodles
with seasoning packet

1 T. olive oil

2 boneless, skinless
chicken breast halves

2 egg yolks

3 T. lemon juice

½ C. butter, divided

Preparation

Remove seasoning packet from noodles and set aside. Heat oil
in a small skillet over medium heat. Add chicken and sprinkle
pieces with about half the seasoning from packet; discard
unused seasoning. Cook chicken on both sides until golden
brown and no longer pink inside. Meanwhile, in a small saucepan
over high heat, bring 2 cups water to a boil. Break up noodles
and add to boiling water; cook for 3 minutes or until tender. In
another small saucepan, whisk together egg yolks and lemon
juice. Place pan over low heat and add ¼ cup butter; cook and
whisk until melted. Add remaining ¼ cup butter; cook and whisk
until sauce* thickens. Divide cooked noodles between two
serving plates and top each with a piece of chicken and half
the sauce.

* Quantity of sauce may be doubled, if desired.

Ricotta Frittata

Makes 6 to 8 servings

Ingredients

2 C. frozen green peas

3 (3 oz.) pkgs. beef or chicken flavor ramen noodles with 2 seasoning packets

1 (15 oz.) container part-skim ricotta cheese

3 eggs, lightly beaten

½ C. milk

½ C. grated Parmesan cheese

¼ tsp. pepper

1 (14.5 oz.) can diced Italian herb tomatoes

Preparation

Preheat oven to 400°. Lightly coat a 9 x 13″ baking dish with nonstick cooking spray; set aside. In a large saucepan over high heat, bring 6 cups water to a boil. Add peas and return to a boil. Break up noodles and add to boiling water. Reserve two packets of seasoning for later use; discard remaining package or reserve for another use. Cook noodles and peas for 3 minutes, stirring occasionally, until just tender. Drain well and set aside. In a separate large bowl, combine ricotta cheese, eggs, milk, Parmesan cheese, pepper and the seasoning from two reserved packets; stir until well blended. Add noodles and peas, mixing gently. Transfer mixture to prepared baking dish and spread evenly. Bake for 20 minutes or until set. Meanwhile, in a small saucepan over medium-low heat, heat tomatoes. After removing frittata from oven, spoon hot tomatoes over the top and cut into squares to serve.

Shrimp & Ramen Foil Packs

Makes 4 servings

Ingredients

2 (3 oz.) pkgs. shrimp
   flavor ramen noodles
   with 1 seasoning packet

½ C. dried mushrooms,
   chopped

20 large frozen shrimp, thawed

½ C. chopped onion

½ C. sliced green onions

½ tsp. crushed
   red pepper flakes

1 qt. vegetable broth

½ C. mirin (or white wine
   with 1 tsp. sugar)

¼ C. low-sodium soy sauce

4 tsp. sesame oil

Preparation

Preheat oven to 400°. Cut four (18″) pieces of aluminum foil.
Break up noodles coarsely and divide them evenly on the
center of foil pieces. Set aside one seasoning packet; discard
remaining packet or reserve for another use. On top of each
serving of noodles, place a portion of the mushrooms and
five shrimp. Layer with onion, green onions, red pepper flakes
and a sprinkling of seasoning from one packet. Pull up sides
and corners of foil to create basket-shaped pouches with an
opening at the top; set aside. In a small bowl, combine broth,
mirin, soy sauce and sesame oil. Pour a portion of the liquid into
each pouch. Seal open edges of each foil pouch, leaving a small
opening at the top for steam to escape. Place pouches on a
baking sheet and bake for 15 minutes.

Seafood Stuffed Peppers

Makes 4 servings

Ingredients

- 2 large or 4 small green or orange bell peppers
- 1 (3 oz.) pkg. shrimp or mushroom flavor ramen noodles with seasoning packet
- 5 to 8 oz. frozen shrimp, thawed and chopped
- ⅓ C. hoisin or stir-fry sauce
- 1½ C. chopped bok choy or green cabbage
- ¾ C. fresh halved snow peas, strings removed
- 4 green onions, sliced
- ¼ tsp. crushed red pepper flakes, optional
- 2 tsp. toasted sesame seeds*

Preparation

Cut large bell peppers in half lengthwise or cut tops off small peppers. Remove membranes and seeds. Fill a large saucepan with water and bring to a boil. Immerse peppers in boiling water for 3 minutes. Remove and drain peppers on paper towels, cut side down. Meanwhile, in a small saucepan over high heat, bring 2 cups water to a boil. Break up noodles and add to boiling water with seasoning from packet. Cook noodles for 3 minutes or until tender. Add shrimp and cook for 30 seconds longer. Drain noodle mixture, discarding liquid; return to saucepan over medium-low heat. Add hoisin sauce, bok choy, snow peas, onions and red pepper flakes; stir and heat though. Arrange bell peppers, cut side up, on a serving platter. Spoon filling mixture into peppers. (Extra filling may be distributed around peppers.) Sprinkle with sesame seeds and serve warm, or refrigerate until chilled to serve cold.

To toast, place sesame seeds in a single layer on a baking sheet. Bake at 350° for approximately 6 to 8 minutes or until sesame seeds are brown.

Variation: *In place of shrimp, use one 6-ounce can crabmeat, drained and shredded.*

Ramen Chicken à la Orange

Makes 2 servings

Ingredients

3 T. orange marmalade

½ tsp. dry mustard

¼ tsp. crushed
red pepper flakes

¼ tsp. pepper

⅛ tsp. salt

2 boneless skinless chicken
breast halves, diced

1 (3 oz.) pkg. chicken
flavor ramen noodles
with seasoning packet

Vegetable oil

Fresh orange slices, optional

Preparation

In a shallow microwave-safe dish, stir together marmalade, dry mustard, red pepper flakes, pepper and salt until well blended. Cover and microwave for 30 seconds or until slightly warmed. Add chicken to dish and stir until well coated; set aside. Meanwhile, in a small saucepan over high heat, bring 1 cup water to a boil. Stir in seasoning from packet. Add block of noodles to water and cook for 3 minutes, stirring to separate noodles. Cover pan and allow to stand until most of water is absorbed. In a large skillet over medium heat, add enough oil to almost coat the bottom. When hot, add chicken mixture and stir-fry for 5 to 7 minutes. During the last 1 to 2 minutes of cooking time, add noodles; continue to stir-fry until chicken is no longer pink inside. Garnish with orange slices and serve promptly.

Ramen-Stuffed Chicken

Makes 4 to 6 servings

Ingredients

1 whole chicken, about 3 lbs.

2 large sage leaves

2 large sprigs rosemary

Vegetable oil

Poultry seasoning

Salt and pepper
to taste, optional

1 (3 oz.) pkg. chicken flavor
ramen noodles with
seasoning packet

Preparation

Preheat oven to 325°. In a small saucepan over high heat, bring 2 cups water to a boil. Reserve seasoning packet for later use. Break up noodles coarsely into boiling water and cook for 2 minutes or until softened. Drain off all but about 1 tablespoon water and return to saucepan; set aside. Rinse chicken inside and out; pat dry. Discard giblets and neck or reserve for another use. Insert one sage leaf and one sprig of rosemary under the skin on each side of chicken breast. Sprinkle poultry seasoning lightly inside the body cavity. Add half of seasoning from reserved packet to cooked noodles and stir to coat; discard unused seasoning. Gently stuff noodles into chicken cavity. Twist wing tips under the back. Place chicken on a rack in a shallow roasting pan, breast side up. Brush outside of chicken with a thin coating of oil; sprinkle additional poultry seasoning and/ or salt and pepper over outside of chicken. Roast uncovered for approximately 60 minutes or until drumsticks move easily, juices run clear and internal temperature of stuffing registers 165° on an instant-read thermometer. If desired, baste with juices several times during cooking. Let stand for 10 minutes before removing stuffing and carving meat.

Pork Bake

Makes 4 to 6 servings

Ingredients

1 lb. boneless pork loin
¼ C. flour
¼ tsp. pepper
2 T. vegetable oil
1 (16 oz.) pkg. frozen bell pepper and onion stir-fry vegetables, thawed
1 (10.7 oz.) can cream of mushroom soup

1 (4 oz.) can sliced mushrooms, drained
2 T. soy sauce
¼ tsp. ground ginger
1 (3 oz.) pkg. Oriental flavor ramen noodles with seasoning packet
¼ C. slivered almonds

Preparation

Preheat oven to 350°. Coat a 2-quart baking dish with nonstick cooking spray; set aside. Trim fat from pork. Thinly slice meat across the grain into bite-size strips. In a medium bowl, stir together flour and pepper. Working in batches, add pork to flour mixture and toss gently to coat. In a large skillet over medium-high heat, heat 1 tablespoon oil. Add half the meat and cook until browned. Remove to a plate to keep warm. Repeat with remaining 1 tablespoon oil and meat. Return all meat to skillet and add vegetables, soup, mushrooms, soy sauce and ginger; reduce heat to low to keep warm. Meanwhile, in a small saucepan over high heat, bring 2 cups water to a boil. Break up noodles and add to boiling water; reserve seasoning packet. Cook noodles for 2 minutes or until almost tender; drain. Add noodles and seasoning from reserved packet to meat mixture in skillet; stir gently to blend. Transfer mixture to prepared baking dish and sprinkle with almonds. Bake uncovered for 35 minutes or until heated through.

Noodles with Lentil Sauce

Makes 4 to 6 servings

Ingredients

½ C. chopped onion

½ C. chopped carrot

½ C. chopped celery

1 (14.5 oz.) can diced tomatoes with juice

1 (8 oz.) can tomato sauce

3 oz. dried lentils, rinsed and drained

½ tsp. dried oregano

½ tsp. dried basil

½ tsp. garlic powder

¼ tsp. crushed red pepper flakes

2 (3 oz.) pkgs. beef flavor ramen noodles with 1 seasoning packet

1 tsp. butter

Preparation

In a slow cooker, mix together onion, carrot, celery, tomatoes with juice, tomato sauce, ½ cup water, lentils, oregano, basil, garlic powder and red pepper flakes; stir well. Cover and cook on low setting for 8 to 10 hours or on high setting for 3 to 5 hours. Before serving, in a medium saucepan over high heat, bring 4 cups water to a boil. Break up noodles and add to boiling water; set aside one seasoning packet and discard remaining packet or reserve for another use. Cook noodles for 3 minutes or until tender. Drain and return to saucepan. Stir in butter and the seasoning from one packet until blended. Place noodles in a large serving bowl and pour lentil sauce over the top; toss to combine. Serve hot.

Side Dishes

Broccoli Casserole

Makes 6 to 8 servings

Ingredients

½ C. mayonnaise

½ C. plain yogurt
(or sour cream)

1½ C. shredded sharp
Cheddar cheese, divided

⅓ C. blue cheese
salad dressing

2 eggs

½ tsp. salt

1 tsp. pepper

1 (3 oz.) pkg. chicken
flavor ramen noodles
with seasoning packet

1 T. butter

12 oz. sliced mushrooms

6 C. chopped fresh
broccoli, blanched*
(or frozen broccoli)

Preparation

Preheat oven to 350°. Coat an 8˝ square baking dish with nonstick cooking spray; set aside. In a medium bowl, combine mayonnaise, yogurt, 1¼ cups cheese, dressing, eggs, salt, pepper and seasoning from packet; stir until well blended and set aside. In a medium skillet over medium heat, melt butter. Add mushrooms and sauté until mushrooms are browned and tender. In a large bowl, combine broccoli and mushrooms. Break up noodles and add to bowl. Pour dressing mixture over broccoli mixture and toss until well coated. Spread mixture in prepared baking dish. Cover and bake for 30 to 40 minutes. Uncover, sprinkle with remaining ¼ cup cheese and bake for 12 to 15 minutes longer to brown. Let stand 15 minutes before serving.

To blanch, bring water to a boil in a large saucepan. Add broccoli and cook 2 to 3 minutes or just until broccoli is slightly tender. Transfer broccoli to a large bowl of ice water to chill quickly. Drain and proceed with recipe.

Sweet 'n Hot Green Beans

Makes 4 servings

Ingredients

1 (3 oz.) pkg. chicken or
beef flavor ramen noodles
with seasoning packet

2 T. butter

1 (15 oz.) can green beans

2 to 3 tsp. brown sugar

2 tsp. hot pepper sauce,
or to taste

Salt and pepper to taste

Preparation

Reserve seasoning packet for later use. In a microwave-safe bowl, coarsely break up noodles. Add just enough water to cover noodles. Microwave for 1 to 2 minutes until noodles separate; drain well and set aside. In a medium skillet over medium heat, melt butter. Add noodles and green beans; stir to coat. Gradually add brown sugar, seasoning from reserved packet, hot sauce, salt and pepper; toss well and cook until heated through. Serve immediately.

Batter Fried Ramen

Makes 4 to 6 servings

Ingredients

2 (3 oz.) pkgs. ramen
noodles, any flavor

3 eggs, divided

1½ C. flour

1 tsp. salt plus more
for seasoning

1 (12 oz.) can beer

4 C. canola oil (for frying)

Preparation

In a medium saucepan over high heat, bring 4 cups water to
a boil. Remove seasoning packets from ramen packages and
discard or reserve for another use. Place blocks of noodles into
boiling water and cook for 3 minutes or until tender. Meanwhile,
in a medium bowl, whisk together 1 egg, flour, 1 teaspoon salt
and beer. In a separate bowl, beat 2 eggs. Place oil in a deep cast
iron pot over medium heat or a deep fryer; heat oil to 350° to
375°. Drain cooked noodles and separate into strands, twisting
lightly; set on paper towels to dry slightly. Dip a few strands at a
time into beaten eggs and then into beer batter. Fry until golden
brown. Season with salt, if desired. Serve with your favorite dip.

Peanut Butter Ramen

Makes 4 servings

Ingredients

2 (3 oz.) pkgs. ramen
    noodles, any flavor
1 T. creamy peanut butter

3 T. soy sauce
2 T. sesame oil

Preparation

Remove seasoning packets from ramen packages and discard
or reserve for another use. In a medium saucepan over high
heat, bring 4 cups water to a boil. Break up noodles and add
to boiling water; cook for 3 minutes or until tender. Drain
noodles and return to saucepan; set aside. In a medium skillet
over medium-low heat, warm peanut butter. When it begins to
melt, add soy sauce and oil; stir until well blended. Add cooked
noodles and toss until evenly coated and heated through.
Serve immediately.

Ramen with Thai Peanut Sauce

Makes 2 servings

Ingredients

1 (3 oz.) pkg. ramen
noodles, any flavor

3 T. creamy peanut butter

2 T. low-sodium soy sauce

½ tsp. ground ginger

1 T. cider vinegar

1 T. sesame oil

½ tsp. maple syrup or sugar

Cayenne pepper to
taste, optional

2 green onions, sliced

Preparation

Remove seasoning packets from ramen packages and discard
or reserve for another use. In a small saucepan over high heat,
bring 2 cups water to a boil. Break up noodles and add to boiling
water; cook for 3 minutes or until tender. Drain and return to
saucepan. While noodles are hot, stir in peanut butter until
melted. Add soy sauce, ginger, vinegar, oil, syrup and cayenne
pepper, if desired; stir gently until well mixed. Divide between
serving plates and garnish with onions before serving.

Curried Ramen

Makes 2 servings

Ingredients

1 (3 oz.) pkg. ramen
noodles, any flavor

1 tsp. curry powder

½ tsp. ground cumin

Crushed red pepper
flakes to taste

Preparation

Remove seasoning packet from ramen package and discard
or reserve for another use. In a small saucepan over high heat,
bring ¾ cup water to a boil. Place block of noodles in boiling
water and cook for 1 to 2 minutes, stirring several times to
separate noodles. Add curry and cumin; stir well and cook
for 3 to 5 minutes longer or until noodles are tender. Divide
among serving plates and add a dash of red pepper flakes
before serving.

Spicy Hot Curry Noodles

Makes 4 servings

Ingredients

3 to 5 Thai chiles or jalapeño
  peppers, minced

1 tsp. minced garlic

¼ tsp. cumin seeds, or to taste

½ to ¾ C. frozen
  mixed vegetables

4 (3.5 oz.) pkgs. curry flavor
  ramen noodles* with
  3 seasoning packets

3 green onions, sliced

Preparation

In a large saucepan over high heat, combine 3 cups water, chiles, garlic and cumin seeds; bring mixture to a boil. Add vegetables and cook for 3 minutes or until slightly tender. Break up noodles and add to saucepan; bring mixture back to a boil. Add seasoning from three packets and stir well; discard remaining packet of seasoning or reserve for another use. Cook for 3 minutes or until noodles are tender and water is reduced to desired consistency. Garnish with onions and serve hot.

One 11.29-ounce package of curry flavor ramen noodles may be substituted.

Italian Noodle Bowl

Makes 4 servings

Ingredients

2 (3 oz.) pkgs. ramen
  noodles, any flavor

2 T. Italian salad dressing,
  or more to taste

Salt to taste

¼ C. shredded
  mozzarella cheese

1½ T. grated Parmesan cheese

Preparation

Remove seasoning packets from ramen packages and discard or reserve for another use. In a medium saucepan over high heat, bring 4 cups water to a boil. Break up noodles and add to boiling water; cook for 3 minutes or until tender. Drain well and return to saucepan. Stir in dressing and season with salt. Transfer hot noodles to a serving dish and sprinkle with mozzarella cheese and Parmesan cheese; let stand several minutes to allow cheeses to melt before serving.

Oriental Noodles

Makes 4 servings

Ingredients

2 (3 oz.) pkgs. Oriental
flavor ramen noodles
with seasoning packets

6 T. low-sodium
soy sauce, divided

2 T. olive oil

1 T. minced garlic, or to taste

2 tsp. prepared yellow mustard

Preparation

Reserve seasoning packets for later use. In a medium saucepan over high heat, bring 4 cups water to a boil; add 4 tablespoons soy sauce. Break up noodles and add to saucepan; boil for 3 minutes or until tender. Meanwhile, in a small bowl, stir together seasoning from both packets, remaining 2 tablespoons soy sauce, oil, garlic and mustard; set aside. When noodles are tender, drain off water and reduce heat to medium. Add sauce mixture to noodles and stir until coated. Serve immediately.

Spicy Skillet Ramen

Makes 1 to 2 servings

Ingredients

1 (3 oz.) pkg. beef flavor
  ramen noodles with
  seasoning packet

2 T. barbeque sauce

1 T. hot pepper sauce

1 T. vegetable oil

⅓ C. milk

Dash of lemon pepper,
  or less to taste

Dash of garlic powder,
  or less to taste

Dash of onion powder,
  or less to taste

½ red onion, diced

Preparation

Empty the seasoning from packet into a small saucepan; set
noodles aside. To saucepan, add ⅔ cup water, barbeque sauce,
hot sauce, oil, milk, lemon pepper, garlic powder and onion
powder; stir well to blend. Place block of noodles into pan to
soak, flipping after several minutes to marinate both sides until
noodles are moist but block is still intact. Meanwhile, heat a
small nonstick skillet over high heat. Add noodle block to pan
and sear until well-browned on one side. Flip and sear other side.
Place saucepan over medium heat and simmer barbeque sauce
mixture. When noodles are seared on both sides, pour sauce
over noodles in skillet to flash boil and evaporate the remaining
liquid so noodles achieve a glaze. Sprinkle onion over noodles
and eat promptly.

Homemade Ramen Noodles

Makes 4 to 6 servings

Ingredients

2 C. flour
½ tsp. salt

4 eggs, lightly beaten
Vegetable oil for frying

Preparation

In a large bowl, stir together flour and salt. Make a well in the center and add eggs and 1 tablespoon water. Stir until dough comes together. On a lightly floured surface, knead dough for 10 to 15 minutes, until elastic. Cover lightly and let dough rest for 30 minutes. On a generously floured surface, roll the pasta dough until very thin, using a floured rolling pin. Add flour as needed to prevent sticking. Use a pizza cutter, sharp knife or pasta machine with an angel hair attachment to cut pasta into very thin strips, about 6″ long. Twirl desired number of strips into small bundles or nests. Allow bundles to dry on waxed paper for 2 hours. In a large skillet over medium-high heat, heat ½ cup oil. Add noodles, a few bundles at a time, and fry quickly, about 3 minutes on each side, until puffed up and light golden brown. Remove noodles to paper towels to drain and cool. Repeat with remaining noodles, adding oil to skillet and adjusting heat as needed. To cook noodles, add to lightly salted boiling water and cook until tender, 6 to 8 minutes. Unboiled noodles may be wrapped well and refrigerated for up to 1 week or frozen for up to 3 months.

Ultra Cheesy Ramen

Makes 2 to 4 servings

Ingredients

2 (3 oz.) pkgs. chicken or
   mushroom ramen noodles
   with seasoning packets
1 C. Cheez Whiz

1 C. shredded Cheddar cheese
2 to 4 T. milk
Croutons, coarsely
   crushed, optional

Preparation

In a medium saucepan over high heat, bring 4 cups water to a
boil. Add seasoning from one packet to water; reserve remaining
packet for later use. Break blocks of noodles in half and add to
boiling water; cook for 3 minutes, stirring several times until
noodles are separated and tender. Drain and return noodles to
pan to keep hot. Meanwhile, place Cheez Whiz in a microwave-
safe bowl and heat in 30 second intervals until warm, stirring
several times. Pour warm cheese over hot noodles in pan. Stir
in Cheddar cheese and half (or all) of seasoning from remaining
packet. Blend in enough milk, 1 tablespoon at a time, to achieve
a creamy consistency; let stand for 1 to 2 minutes to melt. If
necessary, warm in the microwave for 15 to 30 seconds before
serving. Top each serving with crushed croutons, if desired.

*Variations: For added kick, stir in 1 tablespoon butter, ¼ teaspoon
chili powder, a dash of garlic powder, a dash of cayenne pepper
and 1 tablespoon hot pepper sauce before topping with croutons.*

In place of Cheddar cheese, try Parmesan or asiago cheese.

In place of Cheez Whiz, stir in 2 to 3 slices American cheese.

*Browned and seasoned ground beef may be added for
a heartier dish.*

Spanish Noodles

Makes 4 servings

Ingredients

2 (3 oz.) pkgs. chicken
  or picante chicken
  ramen noodles with
  1 seasoning packet

1 to 3 tsp. taco seasoning

1 clove garlic, minced

2 T. finely chopped
  green bell pepper

1 (8 oz.) can tomato sauce

Preparation

Preheat oven to 350°. Lightly coat a small baking dish with
nonstick cooking spray; set aside. In a small saucepan over
high heat, bring ½ cup water to a boil. Break up noodles into
boiling water and stir in seasoning from one packet; discard
remaining packet of seasoning or reserve for another use. Cover
pan, remove from heat and let stand for 4 to 5 minutes or until
noodles soften and water is absorbed. Stir to separate noodles.
Stir in taco seasoning, garlic, bell pepper and tomato sauce until
well blended. Transfer mixture to prepared baking dish and bake
for 20 to 25 minutes or until heated through.

Mock Ramen Alfredo

Makes 4 servings

Ingredients

2 (3 oz.) pkgs. creamy
   chicken ramen noodles
   with seasoning packet

2 T. butter

Dash of garlic powder,
   or more to taste

1 C. small curd
   cottage cheese

¼ C. shredded
   mozzarella cheese

Grated Parmesan cheese

Preparation

Reserve seasoning packets for later use. In a small saucepan over high heat, bring 2 cups water to a boil. Break up noodles and add to boiling water; cook for 3 minutes or until tender. Drain well and transfer noodles to a medium microwave-safe bowl. Add butter, seasoning from both packets, garlic powder and cottage cheese; stir well to blend. Stir in mozzarella cheese. If needed, microwave for 15 to 30 seconds to melt cheese. Top with a sprinkling of Parmesan cheese and serve immediately.

Chinese Fried Noodles

Makes 3 to 4 servings

Ingredients

2 (3 oz.) pkgs. ramen noodles with 1 seasoning packet, flavor of choice

2 to 3 T. vegetable oil

2 cloves garlic, minced

2 T. soy sauce

1 C. frozen corn

½ C. shredded carrots

¼ C. bean sprouts, optional

2 eggs, beaten

½ C. French fried onions, optional

Preparation

Reserve one seasoning packet for later use, and discard remaining packet or reserve for another use. In a small saucepan, bring 4 cups water to a boil. Remove from heat and place blocks of noodles into hot water; cover pan and let stand for 4 to 5 minutes to soften noodles, turning once. Drain well and set aside. In a large skillet over medium heat, heat oil. Add garlic and sauté for 1 minute. Add softened noodles, seasoning from one packet and soy sauce; stir-fry for 3 minutes. Add corn, carrots and bean sprouts, if desired; cook until tender and heated through. Transfer mixture to a plate and keep warm. In the same skillet, cook eggs, scrambling well. Put noodle mixture back into skillet and mix with eggs. Top with fried onions before serving, if desired.

Ramen Pancakes

Makes 8 servings

Ingredients

1 (3 oz.) pkg. ramen noodles
with seasoning packet,
flavor of choice

1 zucchini, shredded

2 green onions, sliced

1 carrot, shredded

2 eggs, beaten

2 T. flour

2 T. vegetable oil

2 T. low-sodium soy sauce

2 T. lemon juice

Preparation

Reserve seasoning packet for later use. In a small saucepan
over high heat, bring 2 cups water to a boil. Break noodles
into four sections and add to boiling water; cook for 3 minutes
or until tender. Drain well. Place cooked noodles in a medium
bowl and add zucchini, onions, carrot, eggs, flour, and
½ teaspoon seasoning from packet; mix gently. Discard unused
seasoning. In a large nonstick skillet over medium-high heat,
heat 1 tablespoon oil. Using half the noodle mixture, make
four pancakes. Fry for 2 to 3 minutes on each side. Repeat with
remaining oil and noodle mixture. In a small bowl, stir together
soy sauce and lemon juice; serve with pancakes.

PDQ Ramen Noodles

Makes 1 to 2 servings

Ingredients

1 (3 oz.) pkg. ramen noodles
with seasoning packet,
flavor of choice

1 T. olive or canola oil

1 tsp. lime or lemon juice

Dash of pepper or
hot pepper sauce

Preparation

Reserve seasoning packet for later use. In a small saucepan over high heat, bring 2 cups water to a boil. Add block of noodles to boiling water and cook for 2 to 3 minutes or just until noodles separate and become tender, stirring occasionally. Drain well. Place noodles in a bowl and add oil, lime juice, half of seasoning from packet and pepper; toss well and serve promptly.

Variation: Stir-fry 1 cup of your favorite vegetables and add to the noodles before serving.

Snacks & Sweets

Ramen Munching Mix

Makes about 5 cups

Ingredients

¼ C. butter

1 tsp. seasoned salt

1 T. Worcestershire sauce

2 (3 oz.) pkgs. ramen noodles, any flavor

2 C. Chex or Crispix cereal

1 C. bite-size pretzels

1 C. roasted or dry roasted peanuts

Preparation

Preheat oven to 250°. In a small saucepan over low heat, melt butter. Stir in seasoned salt and Worcestershire sauce. Remove seasoning packets from ramen packages and discard or reserve for another use. Break noodles into bite-size pieces and place into a large resealable plastic bag. Add cereal, pretzels and peanuts. Drizzle butter mixture over ingredients in bag and seal tightly; shake bag until all pieces are coated. Pour contents of bag into a large roasting pan. Bake for 1 hour, stirring every 15 minutes. Spread on paper towels to cool completely. Store in an airtight container.

Fruity Snack Mix

Makes about 2 cups

Ingredients

1 (3 oz.) pkg. ramen
noodles, any flavor

⅓ C. vegetable oil

¼ C. sliced almonds

½ C. chopped dried
sweetened cranberries

¼ C. diced dried apricots

Preparation

Break noodles into small pieces while still in the package.
Remove seasoning packet from ramen package and discard or
reserve for another use. In a small saucepan over medium heat,
heat oil. Add uncooked noodles and cook until browned, stirring
constantly. Transfer browned noodles to a medium bowl to cool
for 10 minutes. Add almonds, cranberries and apricots; toss well.

Sweet Cinnamon Snack Mix

Makes about 11 cups

Ingredients

2 (3 oz.) pkgs. ramen noodles
5 C. honey graham cereal
3 C. cinnamon flavor
   Teddy grahams
¾ C. sliced almonds

1 C. golden raisins
⅓ C. butter
⅓ C. honey
1 tsp. orange juice

Preparation

Preheat oven to 375°. Remove seasoning packets from ramen packages and discard or reserve for another use. Crush ramen noodles into a large bowl. Add cereal, Teddy grahams, almonds and raisins; stir to combine. In a small saucepan over low heat, melt butter. Blend in honey and orange juice until well mixed. Pour over cereal mixture in bowl and toss to coat. Spread mixture on a 10 x 15″ (or larger) baking pan. Bake for 10 minutes. Let cool.

Sugar 'n Spice Pudding Cups

Makes 6 servings

Ingredients

1 (3 oz.) pkg. ramen
  noodles, any flavor

Sugar

2 eggs, beaten

2 T. butter, melted

1 apple, grated

¼ C. raisins

⅓ C. sugar

½ tsp. ground cinnamon

2 T. bread crumbs

Preparation

Preheat oven to 375°. Remove seasoning packet from ramen package and discard or reserve for another use. In a medium saucepan over high heat, bring 2 cups water to a boil. Break up noodles and add to boiling water; cook for 3 minutes or until tender. Drain noodles and return to saucepan. Meanwhile, lightly coat six (8-ounce) ramekins with nonstick cooking spray; sprinkle with sugar and set aside. To cooked noodles, add eggs, butter, apple, raisins, ⅓ cup sugar and cinnamon; stir until well combined. Spoon mixture into prepared ramekins. Sprinkle bread crumbs on top. Bake for 12 to 15 minutes or until golden brown and bubbly.

Warm-Up Snack

Makes 2 servings

Ingredients

2 (3 oz.) pkgs. spicy chicken or chili flavor ramen noodles with 1 seasoning packet

1 (10.7 oz.) can tomato soup

Hot pepper sauce to taste

½ C. shredded Cheddar, Monterey Jack or American cheese

Preparation

Set aside one seasoning packet and discard or reserve remaining packet for another use. In a medium saucepan over high heat, bring 4 cups water to a boil. Break each block of noodles into four pieces and add to boiling water. Cook noodles for 3 minutes or until tender. Drain well and return to saucepan. Add soup and the seasoning from one packet; stir to blend. Stir in hot sauce and cheese. Serve immediately.

Chocolate No-Bake Cookies

Makes about 3 dozen

Ingredients

3 (3 oz.) pkgs. ramen
  noodles, any flavor

3 T. butter

1 C. semi-sweet
  chocolate chips

1 C. white baking chips

1 C. cashews,
  coarsely chopped

Preparation

Cover a baking sheet with waxed paper; set aside. Remove seasoning packets from ramen packages and discard or reserve for another use. Break noodles into very small pieces. In a large nonstick skillet over medium-high heat, melt butter. Add uncooked noodles and toss to coat. Cook for 3 minutes or until noodles are golden brown, stirring constantly. Remove from heat and transfer to a large bowl; set aside. In a microwave-safe bowl, combine chocolate chips and white baking chips. Microwave in 30 second intervals until melted and smooth, stirring often. Pour melted chocolate mixture over browned noodles. Add cashews and stir until noodles and cashews are evenly coated with chocolate. Drop by teaspoonfuls onto waxed paper. Let cookies cool at room temperature for 30 minutes or until set, or refrigerate to set up more quickly.

Variations: For white no-bake cookies, omit semi-sweet chocolate chips and use 2 cups white baking chips.

Chopped dried fruit, such as cranberries, cherries or apricots, can be stirred into the mixture.

Butterscotch Hay Stacks

Makes 3 dozen

Ingredients

1 (3 oz.) pkg. ramen
noodles, any flavor

2 C. butterscotch chips

1 T. butter

1 T. evaporated milk
(or whole milk)

Preparation

Cover a baking sheet with waxed paper; set aside. Remove seasoning packet from ramen package and discard or reserve for another use. Break noodles into small pieces. In a medium saucepan over low heat, combine butterscotch chips, butter and milk; cook, stirring constantly, until melted and smooth. Add crumbled noodles to saucepan and stir well until coated. Remove from heat. Drop by teaspoonfuls on waxed paper. Refrigerate until set.

Chocolate-Mint Crunchies

Makes 1 to 1½ dozen

Ingredients

1 (3 oz.) pkg. ramen
noodles, any flavor

1 C. dark chocolate
& mint baking chips*

2 to 3 drops
peppermint extract

Preparation

Arrange 12 to 16 miniature muffin cup liners (paper or foil) on a baking sheet; set aside. Remove seasoning packet from ramen package and discard or reserve for another use. Break noodles into very small pieces and place in a medium bowl. Place baking chips in a microwave-safe bowl; microwave for 60 seconds and stir. Microwave for 30 to 40 seconds longer and stir until melted and smooth. Stir in peppermint extract. Pour melted chocolate over noodle pieces and stir well to coat. Working quickly, mound a small spoonful of the mixture into each liner. Let candies cool at room temperature for 30 minutes or until set.

* If combination chips are not available, substitute ½ cup dark chocolate chips and ½ cup mint chocolate chips.

Variations: *Cover a baking sheet with waxed paper. Mix as directed but drop mixture by teaspoonfuls onto waxed paper, flattening to make cookie shapes. If desired, immediately insert wooden popsicle sticks into one edge of each cookie to make crunchies on a stick.*

Screwy Noodle Toffee

Makes 2 to 3 dozen

Ingredients

1 (3 oz.) pkg. ramen
noodles, any flavor

½ C. butter

½ C. brown sugar

1 T. light corn syrup

⅓ C. chopped pecans

Preparation

Preheat oven to 350°. Line a 9 x 13″ baking pan with foil; lightly coat foil with nonstick cooking spray and set aside. Remove seasoning packet from ramen package and discard or reserve for another use. Break noodles into small pieces and set aside. In a small saucepan over low heat, melt butter. Stir in brown sugar and syrup. Increase heat to medium and bring to a boil, stirring constantly; boil for 1 to 2 minutes. Remove from heat. Stir in uncooked noodles and pecans until coated. Spread mixture on prepared foil and bake for 4 minutes. Remove from oven and let cool for 5 to 10 minutes. Chill for at least 1 hour before cutting into bite-size pieces.

Chocolate Faux Tapioca Pudding

Makes 4 servings

Ingredients

1 (3 oz.) pkg. ramen
   noodles, any flavor
½ C. milk chocolate
   ready-to-spread frosting
1 C. milk

Whipped topping
Sliced fresh
   strawberries, optional
Chocolate chips
   or chunks

Preparation

Remove seasoning packet from ramen package and discard or
reserve for another use. In a small saucepan over high heat, bring
2 cups water to a boil. Break noodles into small pieces and add to
boiling water; cook for 4 to 6 minutes or until very tender. Drain
well. Place warm noodles into a blender container; add frosting
and blend on high for 10 to 15 seconds or until mixed. Add milk
and blend on high for 30 to 60 seconds, stopping to scrape
down sides as needed. Spoon into serving bowls and chill for at
least 30 minutes or until set. Before serving, top with a dollop of
whipped topping, some strawberries, if desired, and a sprinkling
of chocolate chips.

Layered Crunch Bars

Makes about 1½ dozen

Ingredients

1 (3 oz.) pkg. ramen
noodles, any flavor

¼ C. butter

1½ T. sugar

1 C. miniature marshmallows

1 C. milk chocolate chips

½ C. butterscotch chips

⅓ C. sweetened flaked coconut

⅓ C. coarsely chopped
pecans or almonds

Preparation

Preheat oven to 400°. Lightly coat an 8″ square baking pan with nonstick cooking spray; set aside. Remove seasoning packet from ramen package and discard or reserve for another use. Crush noodles and set aside. In a small saucepan over medium heat, melt butter. Add crushed noodles and sugar; mix well. Spread noodle mixture in prepared baking pan. Bake for 7 minutes or until bubbly and light brown. Remove from oven and sprinkle top with marshmallows, chocolate chips and butterscotch chips. Return pan to oven and bake for 8 minutes or until marshmallows are puffy and lightly browned. Remove from oven and sprinkle with coconut and pecans. Bake for 3 to 4 minutes longer. Cool slightly and then loosen bars from edge of pan with a knife. Cool completely before cutting.

Variation: Recipe can be doubled for a 9 x 13″ pan.

Just Peachy Ramen Dessert

Makes 6 to 8 servings

Ingredients

1 (15 oz.) can sliced
   peaches with juice
1 C. half & half
   (or evaporated milk)
¼ C. brown sugar (or honey)

1 (3 oz.) pkg. ramen
   noodles, any flavor
½ C. crushed frosted
   flakes cereal
Vanilla ice cream

Preparation

Preheat oven to 350°. Lightly coat an 8″ square baking dish with
nonstick cooking spray; set aside. Drain peaches, reserving
½ cup of juice. In a medium bowl, combine peach juice, half
& half and brown sugar; stir well. Add peaches and toss until
coated. Remove seasoning packet from ramen package and
discard or reserve for another use. Break up noodles and add
to peach mixture; stir until well combined. Pour mixture into
prepared pan and bake for 5 to 7 minutes. Sprinkle cereal on top
and bake for 5 minutes more or until heated through. Serve hot
with scoops of ice cream.

Sweet Chocolate Noodles

Makes 1 to 2 servings

Ingredients

1 (3 oz.) pkg. ramen
noodles, any flavor

¼ C. plus 2 T. brown
sugar, divided

¼ C. chocolate sauce

½ tsp. vanilla extract

Powdered sugar

Whipped cream

1 maraschino cherry

Preparation

In a small saucepan over medium-high heat, combine 2 cups water and ¼ cup brown sugar; bring mixture to a boil. Remove seasoning packet from ramen package and discard or reserve for another use. Add block of noodles to boiling water; cook for 3 minutes or until tender. Drain noodles and return to saucepan. Stir in remaining brown sugar, chocolate sauce and vanilla until combined. Place noodles on a serving plate and sprinkle with powdered sugar. Top with whipped cream and a cherry.

Crunchy Ice Cream Topper

Makes about 1¼ cups

Ingredients

1 (3 oz.) pkg. ramen
  noodles, any flavor

1 T. vegetable oil

1 T. butter

2 T. brown sugar

½ tsp. ground
  cinnamon, optional

Sugar

Caramel ice cream or
  other flavor of choice

Preparation

Remove seasoning packet from ramen package and discard or reserve for another use. In a medium saucepan over medium heat, combine oil and butter, heating until butter melts. Break noodles into small pieces and add to pan; stir to coat noodles well. Cook for 1 to 2 minutes, stirring constantly, until noodles turn light brown. Stir in brown sugar and cinnamon, if desired. Cook for 2 to 3 minutes, stirring constantly, until noodles are glazed and golden brown. Remove from heat and spread on waxed paper. Sprinkle lightly with sugar; gather corners of waxed paper and toss noodles gently to coat in sugar. Sprinkle warm fried noodles on scoops of ice cream. Extra noodles may be cooled completely and stored in an airtight container.

Coconut-Banana Pudding

Makes 6 to 8 servings

Ingredients

3 (3 oz.) pkgs. ramen
   noodles, any flavor

¼ C. butter, melted

2 eggs

⅔ C. sugar

1 (14 oz.) can coconut milk

½ C. sour cream

1½ tsp. almond extract

¼ tsp. ground cardamom

¼ tsp. anise seed, crushed

Salt to taste

½ C. golden raisins

¼ C. crystallized
   ginger, chopped

2 bananas, peeled
   and thinly sliced

½ C. sweetened
   flaked coconut

2 T. sliced almonds

Preparation

Preheat oven to 350°. Coat an 8″ square baking pan with nonstick cooking spray; set aside. Remove seasoning packets from ramen packages and discard or reserve for another use. Place blocks of noodles in a large bowl and cover with hot tap water. Flip blocks over and let noodles soak for 10 minutes or until strands pull apart easily. Drain off water and toss noodles with butter; set aside. In a large bowl, whisk together eggs, sugar, coconut milk, sour cream, almond extract, cardamom, anise seed and a pinch of salt. Add softened noodles, raisins and ginger, stirring until well mixed. Layer banana slices in prepared pan. Spread noodle mixture on top of bananas. Sprinkle with coconut and almonds. Bake for 1 hour 10 minutes or until golden brown and set. Cool for at least 1 hour before slicing.

Index

Soups

Salads

Main Dishes

Side Dishes

Snacks & Sweets